North Finchley and Beyond

Also by Yvonne Peters
"Have You Got Your Irons?" It's a Waaf's Life,
Greenridges Press, 2004

For my brother
DAVID JULES GOLTON
1927–2000

Co-author and the main reason why this
book was compiled

North Finchley and Beyond

Yvonne Peters and David J. Golton

First published in the United Kingdom in 2009
by Greenridges Press

ISBN 978-1-902019-13-0
Produced by
The Choir Press
www.thechoirpress.co.uk

Contents

Acknowledgements

Firstly I would like to say an enormous thank you to my husband Patrick, for his unfailing help and support while I concentrated on the past. I would also like to give my sincere thanks to the following, all of whom gave me their time and assistance whenever I needed it:

Michael Peters, Helen Franklin, Liz Leaper, Fiona Leaper, Joan Golton, Simon Golton, Mary Franks (Mollie) who sadly died just recently, Patricia Clarke, Denise Wraight, Joan Barrett, and Jack and Anne Loader.

Part One: Yvonne

1

The Family: 1923-28

"Tell me the one about you and the Princess and the cat's whiskers."

By the age of three I had heard all my mother's stories about her younger days several times and knew some of them by heart. The one about the Princess was one of my favourites. I scrambled up beside her on the sofa; she put down her knitting and began in her story-telling voice: "It was a cold winter's night in 1923 and I was expecting my first baby very soon."

"That was me!" I interrupted. "I was your first baby, wasn't I?"

"That's right. And as it happened the Princess Royal, the King and Queen's daughter, was expecting her first baby at about the same time. One evening I was sitting by the fire knitting and Daddy was sitting at the table making a crystal wireless set . . ."

"A cat's whiskers set," I corrected her firmly. I much preferred the nickname to its real one.

"All right, a cat's whisker wireless set." (They weren't called 'radios' in the early days.) "When he got it working," she continued, "the first thing we heard was an announcement that the Princess Royal had given birth to a baby boy. I knew my baby—"

"Me!" I interrupted again.

"Yes, you! would arrive soon, so Daddy went off to fetch the midwife. And you were born at half past two the following morning, February ..." she paused and waited.

"The eighth!" I finished the sentence in triumph.

Mother told the story – at my insistence – so many times that I do not now know if what I remember is the scene itself or her description of it afterwards. The wording was always the same and so, apparently, were my interruptions. Until the day when I didn't end the sentence with my usual flourish. After a pause for thought I asked, "Did the midwife bring me?"

In the matter of sex education Mother was ahead of her time. In an age when it was customary to talk of babies being found under gooseberry bushes, or flown to the house by a stork, she believed in telling the truth as much as possible. She said, "No."

"Then where was I before I got born?"

"Inside my tummy."

I am told this reduced me to astounded silence. Mother had fully expected me to ask the obvious follow-up question, "How did I get out?" Or the embarrassing one most parents dreaded even more – "How did I get in there?" But I didn't. I slid down off the sofa wide-eyed and trotted off to fetch Teddy, my beloved bear, and tell him the amazing thing I had just learned.

During her months of pregnancy Mother had been hoping for a quiet, amenable child. If it was a girl, she wanted one she could dress in frilly dresses and make a fuss of. What she got that cold February night in 1923 was a wayward chatterbox who hated frilly dresses from a very early age and showed a strong aversion to being fussed over, or even helped. Mother always swore that the first sentence I strung together when I learned to talk was, "I want to do it my*self*." It was not until 1927 that she had a child whose temperament more nearly matched the one she had dreamed of.

4

When I was born my parents lived in a flat in Tufnell Park. My mother's mother, "Nannie", lived a convenient walk away in Holloway and she frequently came round to give Mother a much needed helping hand. Mother was not strong. She was often ill after my birth and sometimes had to go into hospital. While she was away, or not well enough to look after me, Father took me to stay with Nannie. This arrangement continued after we moved to North Finchley in 1925. Our new home was a three-bedroomed house, one of a terrace of four, with a garden. Why my parents moved so far away from my grandmother, I don't know. Instead of the convenient walk, there was now a bus and tram ride between them and Nannie. This must have made visiting more difficult for the adults, but I loved those journeys. Clambering aboard the tall red bus was the beginning of a thrilling adventure; the clanking of the swaying tram was exciting. When I was small we sat downstairs inside the bus. I have a hazy memory of perching on Father's knee so that I could look out of the window and watch the people passing by.

The stairs to the upper deck curled round the outside of the back end of the bus and as I grew bigger I wanted to climb up and see whatever there was to be seen from the top. Father always said I was too small when I pleaded with him. Until one magic day when I asked as usual, "Am I big enough to go upstairs yet?", and he said, "Yes!" I stumbled over the bottom step in my excitement.

Buses were open-topped then. I was not tall enough to look over the side, but by standing on tiptoe I found I could just see into the upstairs rooms of some of the shops and houses we passed, especially when they had the light on. It was fun trying to see what other people were doing. If only Father would stop holding on to the back of my coat! I tried to push his hand away, protesting loudly that I could stand up by myself, but he said, "Either I hold on to you or we go downstairs." I knew by his voice that he meant it so I had to put up with being treated like a baby.

I enjoyed staying with Nannie: she bought me colouring books and crayons, read me stories from books she kept especially for me and gave me my very own duster to help with the housework. Nevertheless, I was always glad to go home again. After a few days I started asking, "When is Daddy coming to fetch me?"

The answer was usually, "In a day or so," or, "Only one more sleep," or however many nights I still had to wait. But one day she answered, "Daddy's not coming this time; I'm going to take you home instead."

Surprised, I demanded, "Why?" That was my newest favourite word. When you said it you found out all sorts of interesting things you didn't know before.

Nannie said, "I'm coming to stay with you for a while, so we can go home together."

"Can we go upstairs on the bus?" I asked.

"No," said my grandmother, "not this time."

"Why?" I demanded again.

"You're not big enough yet."

"Daddy lets me," I argued.

"That's different," she said.

"Why?"

Nannie didn't answer the question; she started to look cross. I had noticed before that if you said too many "Whys?" grown-ups often did that. Then they told you not to bother them any more. Which is what happened now. I felt aggrieved and muddled. Surely Daddy knew best? Mummy always said he did. Sometimes grown-ups were very hard to understand.

We set off for Finchley the following day. Inside the bus, of course. But Nannie bought me some sweets and let me eat them on the way (something my father would never permit), so I enjoyed the journey after all.

Nannie

There was a big step up to our front door. I remember standing on the front path and looking up, waiting for Mother to answer Nannie's ring on the bell. But it was Father who opened the door, not Mother. She was hanging back, standing by the sitting room door, carrying something in her arms. I mounted the step and went in, not sure what was happening. Mother leaned over to show me what she had in her arms and Father said, "Say hello to your new baby brother."

I have been told I stood looking at the sleeping bundle for several moments before asking, "Did he come out of your tummy, like me?"

Mother said, "Yes" and once more waited for the awkward follow-up questions, but the only one I asked was, "What's his name?"

"David," said my mother.

"That's a nice name," I said, and ran off into the garden to think about this enormous happening on my own.

7

Looking back now, I am surprised that I was eleven or twelve before I learned how babies were created. But it was not during a cosy chat at bedtime, with Mother sitting on the side of my bed, talking in low, confidential tones. We were in the kitchen when she told me. She was standing at the sink doing some washing and I was kicking my heels doing nothing in particular. I have no idea how the subject came up, or exactly what she said, but I do remember my reaction. I was shocked! Mother made me promise not to say anything to my friends at school, not even my best friend, Mollie. I kept my promise, only to discover later that Mollie had known all about it for ages. Her sister-in-law had told her!

Some weeks after David arrived I was helping Mother bath him in the tin bath in front of the fire in the front room (the sitting room). David loved his bath. He jerked his arms and kicked his legs, delighted to be free of his nappy. I joined in the fun, splashing the water about until Mother had to call a halt "before we're soaked to the skin". She held the baby very carefully, with one hand behind his head to stop it lolling back. I wanted to have a go but she said I had to wait until he was a bit bigger. Every day I asked hopefully, "Is he big enough now?" and was disappointed when she still said no.

On this particular morning, having lifted him out of the water and laid him on the warm bath towel draped over her lap, Mother turned to reach for the talcum powder and found she had forgotten to bring it in with her from the kitchen. Wrapping David up in the towel she got up and went to fetch it. I followed close behind to carry the tin back for her. As she opened the kitchen door we saw the door into the garden slowly opening. A man was outside, close to the door with his head bent, listening. We could see his fuzzy outline through the bubbly glass in the top half of the door. It was creepy. Mother stood very still and I held on to her skirt, pressing myself against her. I was not really frightened, I just felt uneasy. The man pushed open the door and stood in the opening. Mother said sharply, "What do you want?"

The man said, "I'm looking for Mr Smith."

Mother snapped, "There's no one called Smith here."

He hesitated, then turned and ran down the garden path to the back gate. This led out into an alleyway that ran past the end of all the terrace gardens. I let go Mother's skirt, and she moved quickly to the back door, shut and locked it and pushed the bolts home top and bottom. Then she handed me the talcum powder from the dresser shelf and we returned to the sitting room. Here she sat down again, unwrapped David from the towel and powdered him all over as if nothing had happened.

There were shouts coming from the road. I climbed up on the arm of the sofa in the bay window to look out and see what was going on. Mother said, "Get down and come away from the window." I didn't obey at once, lingering long enough to see several policemen gathered round the end of the alleyway where it emerged between two houses further down the road. Mother raised her voice, "Did you hear what I said?" Reluctantly I climbed down and went over to stand beside her and watch while she manoeuvred David's arms into his little vest and long gown and matinee jacket. I tried to tell her about the policemen, but she didn't seem interested. I found out what had been happening by eavesdropping when she described the episode to Nannie a few days later.

My grandmother came up to spend a day with us once a week. After dinner, while David had his afternoon sleep, Mother and Nannie settled themselves in armchairs on either side of the sitting room fire and did the mending. And as they darned socks and stockings, replaced missing buttons and patched old pillowcases and things, they gossiped. Meanwhile I played with my toys on the floor.

Most of the time I found their conversation boring, but occasionally, if I crept behind Nannie's chair and kept very quiet, they would forget I was there and talk about something really interesting – such as the man at the back garden door.

Apparently our intruder had been spotted climbing in through a window of a house next to the entrance to the alleyway. The sharp-eyed neighbour, who happened to possess a telephone, rang the police, who arrived just as he emerged from the side entrance of the house. The man had run down the alleyway, probably hoping to escape into the road behind ours, Mayfield Avenue. He was foiled by the high brick wall that separated our alley from theirs. Ours came to a dead end just beyond our back gate and he was trapped. The police had followed him into the alley and he gave himself up.

"You had a lucky escape," said Nannie. "If he was desperate he might have done anything – *anything*," she repeated. The suggestion of horror in her voice made me shiver. I understood for the first time that the situation could have been dangerous. If I had known that at the time I would have been truly scared. As it was, because Mother had shown no fear I had not been afraid. The feeling I remember most clearly is one of frustration at being made to come away from the window and miss all the excitement with the police.

Mother was always cool-headed in a crisis or emergency, which was strange: she worried and fussed endlessly over little things. If she was ever afraid she certainly didn't let it show, not even on the day we had a fire in the cupboard under the stairs.

It happened on a bright Saturday morning in summer when David was about four months old. His pram was out in the back garden and he was fast asleep. I had been told to play quietly, so as not to wake him. But I got bored playing on my own and went into the house to find Mother. I hoped she would play shops with me or something. I opened the back garden door and looked across the kitchen into the hall. The door to the cupboard under the stairs was wide open, blocking my view. I called "Mummy," and she appeared instantly from behind the door looking startled. She hadn't heard me come in. "Go back into the garden and don't come in again until I call you," she ordered.

"Why?" I asked automatically.

"Never mind why, just do as you're told for once." She came towards me almost threateningly; I retreated hastily into the garden followed by Mother's voice shouting "and shut the door behind you!"

I was puzzled and upset. What had I done wrong now? I went over to David's pram and gave it a hard nudge, hoping he would wake up. He stirred, gave a spluttering sigh and settled back to sleep. I didn't dare nudge any harder in case it startled him and he woke up crying.

Father

I wandered down the garden to play on the swing. Time passed. David went on sleeping. Mother didn't come to the door to call me in. Perhaps she had forgotten me? I began to feel tearful. And then the back door opened and Father came out, smiling. Mother's instruction to be quiet flew right out of my head. I yelled, "Daddy!" and jumped off the swing; in my growing misery it had slipped my mind that it was Saturday. For the rest of the week Father didn't get home until my bedtime, but on Saturdays he only worked until one o'clock and Mother delayed dinner until he got home. Shouting "You're back!" at the top of my voice I raced up the garden and threw myself at him. He laughed. "Steady on there, you'll have me over."

David, jerked out of sleep by the noise I was making, heard Father's voice and gave his "I want to be picked up" cry. Mother appeared at the back door to announce that dinner would be ready in about ten minutes. She scooped David up and took him off to make sure he was dry and comfortable before propping him up with cushions in the fireside chair in the dining room. I had followed her into the house and she set me to keep an eye on my brother until Father came in from the garden. There was a strange smell in the hall; it seemed to be coming from the cupboard under the stairs. When Father came in I asked him what it was. "I can't smell anything," he said vaguely. I knew he had a poor sense of smell, so I believed him. I asked Mother when she brought in the dinner. "It's nothing for you to worry about," she replied and immediately asked Father what sort of a morning he'd had, shutting me out of the conversation.

At the first opportunity I determined to look in the cupboard and see for myself what was making the smell. I waited until David was asleep upstairs and Mother and Father were having an after-dinner snooze in the sitting room, then crept towards the cupboard door. It was locked and the key was missing. It was missing the next time I tried, and the next. Finally, as the smell faded, I lost interest and forgot about it.

It was several months before I heard my grandmother refer casually to "the day you had a fire under the stairs."

Fire! We'd had a fire, and I had known nothing about it! I don't know to this day what caused it. The electricity meter was in that cupboard and I suppose it was something to do with that.

David must have been about nine or ten months old when Mother had to go into hospital once more. I was taken down to stay with Nannie as usual, but for some reason David did not come with me. Father was left literally holding the baby. As he told the story later, he was unable to get compassionate leave to stay at home and was at his wit's end to know what to do. Finally, in desperation he took him along to the local orphanage. The Wright Kingsford Home was well known in the district. It was not uncommon to see a crocodile of girls, dressed in their red and black uniform, out for a walk on fine days. One account of the orphanage talks of the children wearing boots, but I can remember seeing them at Tally Ho! Corner walking along bare-footed. The Matron, the Hon. Miss Blanche Wright and her assistant Miss Ellen Kingsford, eyed Father with open suspicion when he arrived on their doorstep with my brother, thinking he was trying to abandon an unwanted baby. Very reluctantly they agreed to take David in until Mother was able to look after him again, but they were clearly not happy. Their relief when Father turned up the following evening to visit the baby was palpable.

Father had left work early to be sure of seeing his son before the children were put to bed. He was shown into a large room where the children were having supper. Those who could feed themselves were seated at a long table. Those who could sit up but could not yet manipulate a spoon were strapped into high chairs. Several young nursery maids were feeding them. Father looked round for David and was mortified to discover that he could not identify him. David was fair with blue eyes – and so were most of the others! To his chagrin Matron had to tell him which child was his! In later years, if Mother was annoyed with David for any reason she would sometimes say, "I think Daddy must have brought home the wrong baby when he collected you." If she had said such a thing to me I would have been deeply upset, but as far as I know it never bothered David in the least. But then, his relationship with Mother was very different to mine. They were, as we would say today, 'on the same wavelength'. Mother and I were not. At that time I got on more easily with Father. In my eyes he was the tallest, the strongest and the cleverest Daddy in the whole world. He was also the most handsome, with dark wavy hair, deep brown eyes and a lovely smile. Whenever Mother read me a fairy story in which the prince was tall, dark and handsome I thought of Father. It is not putting it too strongly to say I idolised him.

He loved making things. When I was about three years old he made me a swing with safety bars so I couldn't fall out. I must have been five when he made me a scaled-down version of an adult's deckchair. That was the day I realised fully for the first time that it was unwise to disobey him. I was thrilled with the chair, except for one thing. Because David was at the crawling stage, grabbing hold of things to pull himself upright, Father had adapted the back of the chair for safety. Instead of the rung across the back fitting into notches cut into the frame, it was held in place by two strong metal spring clips. It could not, therefore, be accidentally dislodged if the chair was pulled sideways. I was sternly forbidden to touch these clips in case I injured my fingers. This meant that the chair always had to be set up for me by an adult. And, as usual, I wanted to do it myself. The bit about hurting my fingers had gone in one ear and out of the other. As soon as Father had gone indoors I was round the back of the chair fiddling with one of the clips to see if I could get it open. The result was predictable. Before I could free the rung the clip snapped shut, trapping my thumb. I howled with pain and fright; Mother came running from the house with Father at her heels. She was horrified to see my trapped hand beginning to swell and put her arms around me to comfort me.

Without saying a word, Father freed my thumb, threw the chair aside and went to the tool shed. Mother took me into the kitchen to bathe my hand in cold water. Then she took me on her lap to kiss my sore thumb better. She also gave me one of her special chocolates from the box Father had given her for her birthday. Father brought his largest hammer from the shed and smashed the little chair to pieces.

I never forgot the incident. When he later made us a see-saw I knew better than to disregard his order: "Use it properly and don't fool about on it."

We were never allowed to play in the street with the other children, but were encouraged to bring our friends in to play. The swing, now updated for older children, and the see-saw proved very popular.

Father was strict, but he could also be fun. Sometimes on Sunday afternoons, while Mother did the washing up after dinner, Father and David and I would join her in the kitchen for a sing-song. Sitting on one of the kitchen chairs, with me on one knee and David on the other, he sang us old music hall songs. One of his favourites had the line in it "Once aboard the lugger and the girl is mine." I asked, "What's a lugger?"

"It's a boat," said Father.

The bit about the girl puzzled me. "Why—?" I started to ask. Mother said, before I could finish my question, "Why don't you sing the one about the toreador?" and Father began, "Oh, list while I tell you of the Spaniard who blighted my life," and Mother joined in. When we came to "He shall die! He shall die! He shall die tiddly-i-ti-ti-ti-ti-ti-ti!" I sang too, at the top of my voice and David gurgled with delight and sang scribble. The lines, "I'll raise a bunion on his Spanish onion if I catch him bending tonight" always reduced me to helpless giggles and David copied me. Neither of us knew what we were laughing at, it just sounded so funny. At the end I demanded, "Sing it again," and David bounced up and down and talked scribble again. Or what sounded like scribble.

My brother started talking when he was about eighteen months old but he didn't speak English until much later. The language he spoke was all his own creation and needed an interpreter to understand. That job usually fell to me. I can only remember one of his words. "Diggle" was a drink of water.

We had all the childhood ailments between us. I probably brought them home when I started school. It was therefore most unfair of fate to decree that I should take everything lightly and David should be really ill when the 'bug' reached him. I had very few spots when I caught chicken pox; David was smothered in them and felt poorly, which I did not. His temperature went so high when he had the measles that he had hallucinations, shouting out in terror at some monster only he could see. My worst discomfort was having to stay in a darkened room in case my eyes were affected. This was extremely frustrating. A patch of ground at the end of the garden was used as a dump. Here Father had his compost heap and made the occasional bonfire. Earlier in the year he had made a flowerbed along one side of the dump and shown me how to plant seeds and look after them when they germinated. I went down every morning before school to watch for the little green shoots to appear above the earth and was thrilled when they grew into healthy plants that produced fat little buds. I couldn't wait for them to open. At which point I got measles and was confined to the darkened bedroom. Mother assured me that my plot was a blaze of colour, but refused to allow me so much as a peek between the drawn curtains to see it for myself. By the time my eyes were pronounced out of danger the best of the blooms were over. I gave up gardening after that. It was too frustrating.

Mumps passed me by; David's face blew up like a balloon. Neither did I get whooping cough. Looking back now I realise that David nearly died. At the time I knew he was very ill but the possibility of his dying never occurred to me. This again was due to Mother's calm attitude. A sheet drenched in Dettol hung across his bedroom door, which was left open for Mother to slip in and out easily whenever she was needed, which was often. I can remember sitting on the stairs listening to her soothing voice murmuring to him as he fought for breath. As an adult he could still recall struggling to inhale the fumes as Mother held his head over a jug of hot water mixed with Friars Balsam.

Another aid to breathing, practised by families who lived near a gasworks, was to take the child along to breathe in the coke fumes. We lived too far from Mill Hill gasworks to do this and I doubt if Mother would have taken such a sick child out of the house even if we had possessed a motor car. It was certainly out of the question by public transport.

Although David survived the whooping cough he was never a robust child. When he was three or four years old he had trouble with his legs. I have forgotten what it was – if I ever knew. He had to wear calliper splints on both legs for twenty-four hours a day every day for months. They reached from his thighs to his ankles, holding his legs rigid. There was a high stone step up from the garden to the back door which he at first had great difficulty in climbing stiff-legged. However, once he got the hang of it and learned how to keep his balance, he managed extremely well. He never complained no matter how much he must have hated the wretched things; he never cried either. In fact in his own account of our early years he doesn't even mention them.

David wearing his calliper splints
with Yvonne and a visitor

2

Keeping House: the 1920s and 30s

According to Mother, when we moved into Finchley Park in 1925 our back garden looked out over a field; North Finchley was semi-rural then. However, developers were already buying up the land for housing, leaving a few small farms dotted about the district. There was one further down Finchley Park on our side of the road, its wide entrance flanked by houses. Standing on my favourite perch – the arm of the sofa – I often watched the cows from the farm being herded up the road to their daytime pastures, the fields between North Finchley and Mill Hill. Their route took them past our house to turn right into the High Road (the Great North Road, now the A1000). Here they ambled along for a hundred yards or so before turning left to go down to the wooden bridge that spanned the Dollis Brook. Their fields lay on the other side. In late afternoon they returned to the farm for the night, using the same route in reverse.

If Mother ever ran out of milk she took a jug down to the farm to buy enough to tide her over. When I was old enough to be sent on short errands by myself she sometimes sent me down instead. From inside the bay window I was very brave about the cows. Faced with the possibility of meeting them on their way back from the fields, I was scared stiff. Anxious to get the errand over and done with as quickly as

Mother, David and Yvonne

possible I scurried down the road and across the yard to the
farmhouse. The farmer's wife was a friendly lady who
chatted away as she took my jug to the dairy. I followed her,
watching as she dipped the long-handled ladle into one of
the tall churns and poured the milk carefully into the jug. I
fidgeted and shuffled my feet, willing her to hurry up, and
turning to leave the second I had handed over the money.
"Just you be careful now! Go slowly or you'll spill it and
have to come back for more," said the farmer's wife. Come
back? I couldn't face even the thought of it! I held the jug
in my two hands and proceeded back home at a snail's pace.
If I had seen the cows turn off the High Road into ours
before I reached our front gate I don't know what I would
have done. Ducked in through someone else's gate and
hidden in their front garden until the danger had passed,
probably. But I never did meet them. It occurs to me now
that Mother would never have sent me out at a time when
the cows were due back. Apart from anything else, having

paid two good pennies (worth under 1p in today's currency) for the milk she would not have risked having it spilt.

There were other interesting things to watch out for besides the cows. The postman delivered three or four times a day: before breakfast, mid morning, early afternoon and after tea. This was especially interesting on birthdays. I would try to beat Mother to the front door to pick up cards, easily recognisable because they would only have a halfpenny stamp on them and were tucked in, not stuck down. It was better still just before Christmas: mysterious packages would arrive, to be spirited away by Mother and "hidden" on top of her wardrobe out of my reach. On Sunday afternoons a man came by with a tray of muffins on his head, ringing a hand-bell to advertise his wares. Mother never bought anything from him; she said it was unhygienic. Every now and then a rag and bone man's horse and cart came up the road. The shabby driver had a very loud and distinctive cry. Mother said he was calling out "Any old iron?", but it didn't sound like it. A knifegrinder sometimes came knocking on doors to ask if we wanted any knives or scissors sharpened. He had a big stone wheel mounted upright on a handcart. When he pumped up and down on a foot pedal the wheel turned and sparks flew as he ran the blades from side to side against its edge. The chimney sweep was very popular entertainment. He carried his tools strapped to a bicycle and I think he towed some sort of small cart behind him to carry away the bags of soot when he had finished. As soon as he stopped outside a house all the neighbourhood children would gather on the opposite pavement to wait for his brush to pop up out of the chimney. Even I, who was usually forbidden to play in the street, was allowed out if the house wasn't too far away and Mother could stand at the front gate and keep an eye on me.

With spring came the return of the "Stop Me and Buy One" man. He sold ice creams from a deep refrigerated metal container mounted on a tricycle and the slogan painted on its side had become his nickname. Every day in summer he pedalled up and down the streets, ringing the bell incessantly to let us know he was coming. Those being the days before refrigerators and freezers were commonplace household items, an ice cream was a real treat.

Our larder, which was an outside extension to the kitchen, faced south. In summer it grew far too warm to keep perishables in and Mother had to improvise other ways of storing them. The sitting room faced north and its tiled hearth was the coolest place in the house. It was here, therefore, that Mother kept the dairy products during the day and anything else that would 'go off' if it got warm. No food could be left there overnight because of the mice. These were probably field mice, dispossessed by the building work going on in their old haunts and delighted to find food in abundance in the houses. Some of them grew very canny about avoiding the mousetraps that were standard items of equipment in every larder.

The sitting room hearth was not ideal, but it was the best option available. Milk was kept by standing the bottle or jug in a bowl of cold water and covering it with a cloth. This absorbed the water and kept the milk cool by evaporation. It worked quite well as long as the water in the bowl was changed as soon as it began to warm up. Even so, the milk frequently 'turned'. It was then poured into a basin. When it had thickened, Mother spooned it into a muslin bag which she hung from the saucepan shelf over the kitchen sink. Once the whey had dripped out she mashed up the solid curds with a little salt to make cottage cheese. Nothing was ever wasted in our house. One way of avoiding refrigeration problems was to buy perishable food in small quantities. This was not difficult to do. The milkman made two deliveries a day, the first very early, in time for breakfast, the second in the afternoon before tea. The baker and the greengrocer called every other day. All the horses knew their rounds as well as the men did, and would move from house to house of their own accord. People, especially children, often came out to give them a carrot, a piece of apple, or a biscuit. One lady came out regularly every day. This caused a real problem when the family went away on holiday. The milkman's horse would stand stubbornly outside the empty house and it took tougher persuasion than the usual "clicking" sound to make him move on.

The butcher's boy called early every morning on his bike, a trade bike with a large basket at the front. Having taken the order for the day, he returned with the meat in time for it to be cooked for lunch (which we called dinner). I don't remember a fishmonger calling; Mother had to go nearly to Tally Ho! Corner, about half a mile down the High Road to the South, to buy fish.

Between our road and Britannia Road, the next turning off the High Road going north, stood a short parade of shops. The one on the corner of Britannia Road sold dairy produce among an assortment of groceries and a small range of household cleaning products. "An absolute godsend" Mother called it if she ran out of something unexpectedly.

Another shop had been turned into a transport café, very popular with carters. They turned their horses and carts into Finchley Park and left them while they went into the café for a meal. There were sometimes two, occasionally three, teams parked one behind the other at the top of the road. We had to pass them every time we went to the shop and back. Normally I was not afraid of horses. The milkman's horse was a particular friend of mine. If I held my hand out flat with a piece of carrot on it he would take the offering gently with his thick lips and stand still while I stroked his nose. But the carters' horses were different. They were much larger, for a start. Once they reckoned they had waited long enough for their driver to return, some of them stamped their big hairy feet, shook their manes and tossed their heads, jangling their harness. To me they looked wild and dangerous. When I went to the shop with Mother I was wary but not really afraid of them, as they obviously didn't bother Mother. She said, "They won't hurt you. Just walk along in the normal way. Take no notice of them and they won't take any notice of you." It worked all right when I was with Mother, but when she started sending me to the shop on my own, fear took over and her advice went right out of my head. The pavement was quite wide at that point and I crept along close to the high wall of the end house, keeping as much space between me and the monsters as possible. The horses shuffled sideways in the shafts, trying to get a closer look at me, making me even more afraid. No doubt they were merely bored and mildly curious about this small human behaving so oddly, but this never occurred to me as a child.

I enjoyed going to the shop with Mother. A shelf in front of the counter held a row of large square biscuit tins with glass lids. These were tilted at just the right angle for children to see the biscuits and pester their mothers to buy some. I have forgotten the shop lady's name, probably because I always thought of her as 'the lady'. In my eyes she looked old, but I doubt now if she was out of her forties. When I was with Mother she was all charm and smiles. Usually she gave me a free biscuit from the tin of my choice. This always tasted so much better than the identical biscuits in our tin at home.

When I was sent on my own, however, the charm soon disappeared. It faded on the day I was sent to buy four eggs. The lady took them from the tray on the counter and put them in a paper bag. I paid for them and carried them home with care. Mother took them out of the bag one by one to inspect them. "This one's cracked," she announced. And so it was. Not badly, but the shell definitely had a hair crack in it. "You'll have to take it back," she said. Cracked eggs cost less than the others, but Mother always paid the higher price for perfect specimens.

The smile left the lady's face when I held out the bag with the one egg in it and told her why I had brought it back. "You must have cracked it on your way home," she said, making no move to take it from me.

"No I didn't," I assured her. By chance there were no teams of horses parked in our road to distract me that day. I had been able to concentrate entirely on the eggs. I was certain the crack was none of my doing. I put the bag on the counter. I thought I would be in trouble if I took it home again. For some seconds the lady stood looking sternly down at me and I stared mutely back, unsure what to do next. Then she took the egg out of the bag to check it before putting it back in the tray and giving me another one. "I'll change it just this once, but next time be more careful," she admonished. I wanted to protest that I had been careful this time, but did not have the courage. I decided I didn't like the lady any more.

From then on I went to the shop reluctantly, braving the horses if there were any there and getting the errand over as quickly as possible. The lady was pleasant enough but I no longer trusted her smile. And I was never again offered a free biscuit from the tins in front of the counter.

The worst trip I ever made to the shop also concerned an egg. Mother sent me to buy three. To my relief there were no teams parked at the top of the road; the errand went smoothly. Some time later Mother started to make a cake. She never cracked eggs straight into the mixing bowl, but broke them into a cup first, to make sure they were fresh. The second one certainly wasn't. It smelt horrid. "You'll have to take it back," said Mother. Remembering how cross the shop lady had been when I returned the cracked egg I asked, "Can't you do it?"

"No," said Mother, "I haven't got time."

I asked, "Why not?"

"Because David's asleep and it would take too long to get him up and ready to go out."

I made another desperate attempt to wriggle out of going. "Couldn't you go on your own? I'll look after David."

"No," said Mother firmly in the tone of voice that warned me to stop arguing.

I took the cup with an ill grace and went. To make things worse, two loaded wagons had arrived at the top of the road since my first trip. Each had a massive horse in front of it. As I drew near them, holding out the cup at arm's length to escape the smell of the egg, first one horse then the other strained towards me. They tried to step up on to the kerb, stretching out their long necks in an effort to see what was in the cup. They thought I was offering them some juicy titbit to eat. And I was terrified.

At the shop I held the cup out over the counter and said politely, "Mummy says please could you take this one back and give her another one," and I added another "please" for good measure.

The lady said coldly, "That's not one of mine. Your Mother must have made a mistake and given you an old one."

"No, she didn't." I was indignant. "We hadn't got any eggs."

Another customer came into the shop and the lady turned to serve her, ignoring me. I put the cup down on the counter and waited. It turned out that the new customer wanted several things and I had to wait some while before she left. By this time the smell of the rotten egg filled the shop. Another customer came in. Even if the lady could ignore my presence again, she couldn't ignore the egg. She took another one from the tray on the counter, put it in a small bag and handed it over with an icy smile. "Here you are.

And take the other one back with you. I don't want it."

My relief at having got another egg was spoilt by the knowledge that I now had to pass the horses again. However, when I turned the corner into our road I saw that the drivers had come out of the café and were getting the wagons ready to move off. Both horses ignored me completely.

"Good girl," said Mother when I handed her the bag. "Was she all right about it?"

"Yes," I lied. If I had told the truth I could see Mother storming round to the shop to have words with the lady for accusing her of being dishonest. Suppose the lady said I was lying? My imagination cringed at the trouble it would cause. Much better to keep quiet. I didn't mention the horses, either. As I had not followed her advice, I was not sure she would be sympathetic. I kept my fear to myself, but I had nightmares about those horses for months.

Mother did her main weekly shopping at the International Stores in the High Road, on the corner of Torrington Park. She had an order book, and provided this was either handed in at the shop, or put through their letter box early in the week, the goods would be delivered a few days later. All Mother had to do was check the order was correct and pay the van driver. "Taking in the book" became my job once I was old enough to go to school by myself as I had to pass the shop on the way. The International became a self-service store some time in the 1960s but they continued their delivery service to their old regular customers for as long as it was needed. By this time the van man had become a friendly lady who came in for a cup of tea and a chat while Mother checked the order.

If shopping was easier in those days, housework was certainly harder. Mother possessed few labour-saving devices. Most chores were done with "elbow grease". Our floors were covered with linoleum. The dining and front rooms had a large square of carpet in the centre of the floor leaving the lino showing round the edges. The carpets were brushed on hands and knees with a stiff hand brush, raising a fair amount of dust in the process. Much of it settled on the lino, which then had to be dusted. Mother used a long-handled mop, shaking it out of the back door or the nearest window when it became clogged up. It was surprising how much gossip she picked up from passers-by while shaking her mop or duster out of the windows.

All the rooms had fireplaces in them. The grates and their arched surrounds needed regular black-leading to prevent them going rusty. Downstairs there were hearthrugs in front of the fireplaces and upstairs each bed had its own rugs or mats beside it. These were taken out into the garden, thrown over the washing line and beaten with a special beater made of woven cane. Mother's was shaped like a large clover leaf with a long "stalk" for the handle. The small slip mats outside each door were taken out and banged against the coal shed wall. These mats could be dangerous, even lethal on occasion. A young friend of Mother's was very proud of her new house when she got married. She polished everything enthusiastically – including, unfortunately, the lino under the slip mats. Her husband skidded on the one outside their bedroom door, fell down the stairs, broke his neck, and died.

Besides daily mopping, all the lino needed regular wax polishing or it cracked. The stairs had a strip of carpet running up the middle, held in place by stair-rods made of either brass or wood. Ours were wooden, but either way the rods were removed and polished once a week. The parts of the treads left exposed on either side of the carpet strip were painted. Mercifully they needed little more attention than dusting. Dust was the bane of the housewife's life, especially in winter when the fires were lit downstairs. They caused a lot of extra dust. They also made extra work. The cinders had to be shovelled from the grate each morning and the ashes brushed out from under it. The fire was then re-laid with crumpled newspaper and sticks or firelighters and the coal carried in for the next fire.

There being no heating in the house apart from the downstairs fires, the furniture acquired a damp bloom unless it was given a wax polish once a week. I remember Mother going from room to room carrying her "housemaid's box" containing dustpan, brushes, tins of polish, polishing rags and dusters, "Zebbo" black-lead and "Brasso" for the bathroom taps.

Fires were only lit in the bedrooms if someone was ill in bed. The exception was Christmas morning. David and I hung pillow cases from the end of our beds on Christmas Eve, anticipating that we would get many more exciting packages than would fit into the traditional sock. Knowing that there would be no more sleep once we had woken up on Christmas morning, our parents encouraged us to drag our bulging 'sacks' into their bedroom to open our presents. This usually happened at some unearthly hour when the room was freezing cold. The fire was a special treat for the whole family.

In really cold weather ice formed in weird patterns on the inside of the windows. Everyone went to bed with a stone hot-water bottle. One morning Father felt something move down by his feet. He threw back the bedclothes and found a mouse had crept in for warmth. He trapped it in the sheet, picked it up by its tail and took it downstairs to dash it against the coal shed wall and kill it. But he didn't look too happy about it. Later I heard Mother, who loathed mice, make a half-joking remark about "the great war hero who couldn't kill a mouse", so I guessed he had let it go free.

I think it was probably after David was born that Mrs Blake started coming in to help with the heavy house-work – the "rough", as it was called. She was a fairly tall, grey-haired woman, older than Mother, with a hard, set face and no time for children. On one of her early visits, when I was hanging around in the kitchen talking to her while she scrubbed the floor, I was brusquely told to get out from under her feet and let her get on with her work.

The weekly washing was not such hard work then as it had been at my grandmother's house. That had a scullery with a large brick-built tub in one corner. This was lined with copper, which gave it its name, and had to be filled by hand using buckets of cold water drawn from the tap over the scullery sink. It was also emptied by hand with a "dipper", a metal bowl with a wooden handle. The water was heated by lighting a fire in the grate built into the bottom of one side of the tub. Modern coppers were freestanding. They were made of zinc, but kept their old name out of habit. Ours stood in the kitchen next to the stone sink. It still had to be filled and emptied by hand, but the water was heated by a gas ring fitted underneath it. Nevertheless washing was still a lengthy, laborious process.

Not everything went into the copper. Mrs Blake stood on a wooden slatted duckboard at the sink to do the rest. Very dirty items were scrubbed on a ridged washboard using a brush and a bar of household soap. When the washing had been rinsed in the sink and put through the heavy wooden mangle that stood outside the back door (we didn't have a scullery), the whites were given a blue rinse, and mangled again. A Reckitt's bluebag dipped in the water made them look even whiter than they were. In an age when a housewife was judged by the whiteness of the washing on her clothes line, this was considered indispensable.

Starch was made up in advance by mixing Robin's starch powder in a bowl of boiling water to the desired consistency. Items to be stiffened were immersed in the cooled mixture and they too were wrung out for a second time – third, if they had also had the bluebag treatment. For this final rinse the sheets and pillowcases were folded carefully, to cut down on the ironing.

Ironing was not considered "rough" work, to be done by Mrs Blake. It was Mother's job. In the early days she used flat irons, heating them on the gas stove. To find out if they were hot enough she spat on the plates. If the spit sizzled they were ready for use. When electric irons came out they were considered a great step forward in technology. Mother plugged hers into the light socket to heat up, having first climbed on a chair to remove the bulb. The early irons having no thermostat, she continued with the "spit and sizzle" method of testing it for heat as before.

As an alternative to doing the washing at home, some people employed a washerwoman who collected it, took it back to her own home to be laundered and return it starched and ironed. She transported the washing either in an old pram or home-made cart of some sort. A popular method of dealing with such items as sheets and pillowcases, etc., was to soak them in a large tin bath, treading out the dirt in the manner of the old-style vineyard workers treading the grapes. But with the spread of commercial laundries, these old practices gradually died out. The laundries collected the dirty washing one week and returned the clean laundry the following week when they collected the next lot. Large flat cardboard boxes and fresh laundry lists were provided for convenience.

To do the housework Mother dressed in what was virtually the housewife's morning uniform: an all enveloping wrap-around pinafore over her oldest clothes, with a clean duster or cotton scarf tied round her hair to keep out the dust. Pinny and headgear were always removed and tossed out of sight in the kitchen if she was called to answer the front door. Likewise they were discarded if she went out into the front garden, even if it was only to pull out a few weeds.

After lunch Mother changed into a more presentable frock. Wearing working clothes in the afternoon was simply "not done". Women had surprisingly strong feelings about this. During the Second World War an office colleague of one of my aunts was bombed out one Sunday afternoon, leaving her literally with only the clothes she stood up in. "And what she was doing in her overall on a Sunday afternoon, I can't imagine," said my aunt. This did not denote a lack of sympathy. She was merely putting into words the attitude prevalent at the time: there might be a war on, but standards were expected to be maintained whenever possible. Especially on a Sunday.

This attitude persisted for some years after the war. When a friend of David's, a doctor, was demobbed from the Navy, he bought a large old house locally to set himself up in practice. During the war he had married Mary, a nurse, who was determined to make as good an impression as possible on their adopted neighbourhood. Decorating materials were in very short supply at that time. She therefore had to be content with giving the place a good spring clean. She started with the hall, which was to do duty as the waiting-room for the immediate future. Being anxious to get the job finished as quickly as possible, Mary worked on into the afternoon. She was still in her working gear when the doorbell rang. Her first instinct was to keep quiet and pretend she was out, but mindful that it could be someone in trouble she answered the door at once. Outside stood a well dressed, imposing lady with a cut glass accent. In commanding tones she asked to speak, not to Doctor W, but to his wife! Trying not to look dismayed, Mary said she was sorry but Mrs W was out: could she take a message? And she solemnly took a message to herself, promising to deliver it as soon as Mrs W returned.

The doctor was not at all pleased when his wife told him what had happened. He said she would look an utter fool if she met the woman again and was recognised. But Mary was not convinced. She thought it was unlikely that the caller would identify anyone she met socially as the charlady who had answered the door. And even if she did, she would probably understand perfectly why Mary had acted as she did. She might even secretly applaud her presence of mind.

3

School: 1928-33

I started school in 1928. Being Roman Catholics, my parents had automatically turned to the local Convent School, St Michael's, in Nether Street. The Convent itself was an attractive old house called The Grange. Set at right angles beside it stood the school: large, rectangular and plain, built of stone. A row of four small Victorian villas abutted the school building and had become part of it. The buildings, together with the extensive grounds surrounding them, were enclosed by a high brick wall. The entrance gate, as high as the wall, was always kept locked. Callers had to ring a bell to be admitted. At that time a nun had to walk down the drive from the Convent to answer the summons. Later a lodge was built inside the gate with a nun permanently on duty as gatekeeper. I was a day-girl at the Convent for eleven years and look back on it with great affection.

It was a lovely summer's day when Mother took me for a preliminary interview with the Headmistress, Sister Patricia. To my eyes she looked tall and stern. I was overawed and knew I had to keep on my very best behaviour. I assume she showed us over the school, but I have no memory of the visit. I know she took us on a brisk tour of the grounds. I can see her now, striding along a path between rows of gooseberry bushes, her veil flapping about behind her. Mother kept pace by her side; I trotted along in the rear. Every now and then I drifted behind and had to run to catch up.

I can also remember a vast lawn, in a far corner of which stood a little wooden house, about the same size as our garden shed at home. It had a sloping roof that stuck out over the doorway and a veranda. I thought it was a playhouse and hoped we would pass close enough for me to look inside. However, as we drew nearer I could see bees flying round it. Hundreds and hundreds of them. The noise of their buzzing grew so loud it was scary. The "house" was in fact an outsize beehive! To my relief the Sister changed direction and avoided it.

There was also a rose garden and an orchard. Eventually, after what seemed an awfully long walk, the path led us under some tall trees and came out on another lawn, much smaller than the first one, in front of The Grange.

The tour ended in a large glass room on the outside of the house (a conservatory, Mother told me later). It was shady with tall plants and palm trees growing in big pots. I had never seen a room like it; I was fascinated. The back wall was covered in green climbing plants and – most fascinating of all – at the foot of this wall was a pond in the floor. It was edged with more plants, some actually growing in the water. Huge goldfish swam idly round, gliding between the stalks. White iron garden chairs and tables stood among the pots and Sister Patricia invited Mother to sit down while they finished their talk. I stood by the pond watching the goldfish, mesmerised. I was looking forward to coming to see them again, but when I started school in the September I learned that all the places we had seen on our visit, including the conservatory, were out of bounds.

The school colours were navy-blue and gold. The official uniform shop was expensive, so my parents made most of my uniform at home. Father made my navy coat, the box-pleated tunic and the shantung blouses; Mother knitted the navy cardigan and woolly gloves. The only things bought from the shop were the navy po-shaped velour hat, the blue-and-gold striped hatband, the hat badge and tie and the woven striped girdle.

It was roughly a mile between home and the school with the busy High Road to cross on the way. I suppose Mother took me to school herself on my first morning, but I can't recall anything at all about my first day there. It must have been difficult for her to get David dressed and in his pram early enough to get to school on time. She soon arranged for an older pupil who lived nearby to collect me in the morning and take me along with her. My escort was a kindly girl, but after a month or so I felt far too grown-up to need watching over. It was a great relief to both of us when I was deemed old enough to walk by myself.

The school taught girls from the age of five to sixteen. Some, whose parents lived abroad, were boarders. Boys were accepted up to the age of eight and the early classes were mixed. I had been secretly afraid of getting lost in what I thought of as a big school, but I needn't have worried. The infants' small world was mainly confined to the Villas. We did not use the main school entrance, we used the front door of one of these villas and our cloakroom had once been somebody's living room. Here the pegs for our coats and hats were set at a convenient height for small people and there was a low bench to sit on while we changed our shoes. House shoes were obligatory, and had to be changed every time we went out to play.

When the Convent acquired the Villas their front gardens had been gravelled over to make a play area for the infant girls. The boys played on what had been the back gardens, now concreted over, except for an area of grass at one end where there were a couple of swings. The side wall of the end villa was so close to a wall of the school that a connecting door had been put in leading straight from our cloakroom to the downstairs corridor, where the junior classrooms were situated.

I had not been at the school for many weeks before Mother was comparing it unfavourably with her own Convent School in Holloway. She said her nuns commanded more respect and maintained stricter discipline than those at St Michael's. I could not understand what she was talking about. We always had to give them right of way if we met them in the corridor and stand up and answer politely when we were spoken to in class. And when the Reverend Mother Superior came over from The Grange to visit the school we were lined up on either side of the corridor and girls had to bow their head while the boys saluted as she passed by. No one could ask for more respect than that, surely? As for the discipline, I was having enough trouble with what we already had, without wanting any more.

The first two classes, Kindergarten and Transition, shared a large classroom between them. In the Kindergarten a lay teacher taught us our letters and numbers, which we practised in sand trays. These were shallow wooden boxes, about the size of seed boxes, with a layer of sand in the bottom. Using our forefingers, we traced our numbers in the sand, shook the tray to smooth the surface again and repeated the exercise until they were, if not perfect, at least recognisable. I got into trouble in one of these early lessons. One of the boys was teasing me and I grabbed a handful of sand from my tray and threw it at him. The teacher was rightly angry. As she pointed out, if it had gone into his eyes the consequences could have been very serious. My punishment was to stand out at the side of the class for the rest of the lesson.

The only other time I can recall getting into trouble in the Kindergarten was due to a misunderstanding. We were being taught the basic beliefs of the Christian Faith and were learning about God the Father, God the Son and – I thought she said – God the Holy Goat. I got the giggles and once more had to stand out of class. Whether this was for showing disrespect to God, or because giggles are infectious and the class was disrupted, I don't know.

These could not have been the only occasions I got into hot water. Persistent offenders were sent to the Headmistress to be reprimanded. If this did not work Sister Patricia sent for your mother! No mother was pleased at being sent for. Mine was furious when it happened to her. I can't recall the interview itself, but I do remember her striding home angrily afterwards while I scrambled along, hanging on to David's high pram to keep myself upright and howling at the top of my lungs.

The end of the Christmas term was marked by an Open Day for parents, with an exhibition of our best work produced during the term. I was proud when my plasticine cake was chosen as an exhibit. Some of the girls were singled out to act as guides to the visitors and show them around our section of the school. For this they were issued with fairy costumes of some flimsy material, with gauze wings in pretty pastel colours. I was not among those selected and felt snubbed and hurt.

Mother said it was ridiculous, having children running about the draughty corridor for hours with next to nothing on in the middle of winter. Someone could catch their death of cold. Even if I had been chosen she would not have let me do it. When one of the fairies caught a chill while on duty and had to stay at home in bed for several days afterwards, I felt a lot better. Obviously, Mother knew best.

At first Mother came to meet me every afternoon, with David in his pram. After a while she took turns with two ladies she met at the school gates, both of whom lived in our direction. Their daughters were my first school friends. Sadly one died of meningitis at the age of eight. The other girl and I remained friends on and off for years, largely I think because we lived near each other and our mothers were friends. Then her family moved away and the friendship petered out.

Towards the end of the Easter term one of the nuns told us the story of the Crucifixion. We listened horror-struck as she described the events leading up to Christ's death on the Cross. One boy shouted out that if he'd been there he would have got a gun and shot all the soldiers dead. It was a comfort to know that Jesus won in the end by rising from the dead on Easter Day.

We duly tried to give up sweets for Lent and made extra efforts to bring pennies to help the black babies climb the stairway to Heaven on the chart pinned up on the classroom wall. The going rate was a penny a stair and there were thirty stairs to the pearly gates. This added up to half-a-crown – five weeks' pocket-money as far as I was concerned. I got 6d a week (two and a half pence in today's money). I don't suppose I was the only one to beg pennies from my mother to help the black babies on their way. At the end of term we went home reckoning up on our fingers how many chocolate eggs we were likely to be given on Easter Sunday.

At dinnertime only day-girls who lived too far away to get home and back in the allotted time stayed at school to eat in the boarders' dining room in The Grange. I became a temporary dinner-girl if Mother was ill, as sometimes happened. I didn't like those days. The only good thing about them was that when we had finished dinner we went out to play in the back playground and could use the swings. For the rest, it felt strange being away from home all day and I didn't think much of the food. It didn't taste nearly as good as Mother's. Most of the time, anyway. Apparently there were exceptions. According to Mother, I once greeted her on my return home with, "We had some lovely soup today. It was brown and thick, with chewy lumps in it," and demanded, "Why can't we have soup like that at home sometimes?"

For the summer term the uniform changed to gold-coloured cotton dresses, navy-blue blazers with the school badge woven into the breast pocket, po-shaped panama hats and white cotton gloves. Winter or summer, gloves were compulsory wear outside the school gates at all times. Prefects stood at the gate to make sure we were wearing them when we went out. If we were ever seen in the street without them we were reported to Sr Patricia.

Father could not make a blazer, but he did make my dresses. He was adept at making clothes that would last, clothes for growing into. Side seams could be let out, waistlines dropped and four-inch hems let down almost indefinitely. My hats started out several sizes too big and had layers of tissue paper stitched inside the lining to pad them out. Final adjustments could be made by sewing on the blue and gold hatband tightly at first and loosening it as required. The only trouble, from my point of view, was that by the time my clothes finally fitted me comfortably, they were nearly worn out!

We all knew the story behind the miniature picture on our school badge. It depicted an angel with sword poised to strike downwards. Beneath it were the words "Quis ut Deus?" – Who is Like to God? Apparently the Devil, Lucifer, had once been a powerful Archangel in Heaven, so powerful that he began to believe himself God's equal. St Michael, another great Archangel, took up his sword and with the cry of "Who is like to God?" drove Lucifer out of Heaven for all eternity. Since his defeat the Devil has wandered the world tempting people to sin in the hope that they would die unrepentant and so join him in Hell.

I'm not sure at what stage we were given our House colours. The School was divided into four Houses: Blue,

Green, Red and Gold. I was assigned to the Blue House. Our patron saint was St Thomas Aquinas and our motto "Veritas" – Truth. A chart hung on the wall in every classroom listing the names of the girls in that form and noting which House they each belonged to. There were also two columns beside the names. One was for points gained, shown in black, the other for points lost, shown in red. Each week the House Prefects came round to inspect the charts, congratulate the winners of black points and reprove the sinners who had accumulated red ones.

Our formal schooling began in Form 1. Sr Mary Michael was the form mistress. She was stockily built with a rather strident voice which became even louder when she got cross. This happened more often with the girls than with the boys. To me she seemed as fearsome as our patron saint. My brother David, who followed me through her class five years later, did not think of her as formidable at all.

Catholic children made their First Holy Communion in Form 2 at the age of eight, before the boys moved on to their own school. It took place during the eight o'clock Mass on the first Sunday after the Feast of Corpus Christi in June. It was preceded a few days earlier by our first Confession. We were prepared for both Sacraments by Sr Mary Michael. She introduced us to the mysteries of the confessional at St Alban's Church, opposite the Convent, instructing us how to address the priest when he opened the little grille in the partition between his seat and the kneeling penitent. The sins, of course, we supplied for ourselves. There were stories told of children who failed to grasp the point of Confession. Feeling that this solemn occasion called for something more impressive than "I disobeyed my mother/teacher", or "I hit my little brother", they took inspiration from the Ten Commandments and confessed to anything from adultery or murder to coveting their neighbour's ox. But I don't think this happened often. And certainly never after Sr Mary Michael's preparation classes! On First Communion morning we assembled at the school at half past seven, to be joined by Catholic children from other schools in the district. Sr Mary Michael lined us all up in crocodile formation and shepherded us across the road to the Church, with other Sisters bringing up the rear. Self-conscious in our white dresses and veils, we followed her up the aisle, past the crowded pews to places reserved for us at the front.

The priest stood with his back to the congregation in those days. After the Consecration of the hosts he took Communion himself and then gave it to the altar boys kneeling on either side of him on the altar steps. Only the priest was allowed to touch the consecrated hosts. As he approached them each boy in turn extended his tongue to receive a sacred host directly into his mouth. Meanwhile we were ushered from our pews by the nuns to line up in rows at the altar rail. The front row knelt down. The big moment had come. The priest turned towards the congregation, descended the altar steps accompanied by the head altar boy and moved to one end of our line. As with the boys, so with the communicants: murmuring *"Corpus Christi"* – The Body of Christ - the priest placed a host on each extended tongue while his attendant held a silver plate beneath each chin to catch any fragment that might inadvertently fall.

The general congregation came up to the altar rail as the last of the children stood up to return to their seats. As only the priest could give Communion it could take what seemed a very long time before that part of the ritual ended. It was compulsory at that time for anyone intending to take Communion to fast from the previous midnight. Not even a drop of water was allowed. Our family had had to make a very early start to get to the Convent by seven thirty. Even on ordinary days the walk to school felt long: on this special day, with an empty tummy, it felt even longer. Mass lasted an hour or more, depending on how many of the congregation lined up to take Communion. This being First Communion Sunday, they all went. At some time towards the end of Mass I remember feeling dizzy and the Church suddenly got dark. Sr Mary Michael hissed at me, "Put your head between your knees" just in time to stop me slipping to the floor. Luckily, it was the custom for the First Communicants to go back to the Convent for breakfast, so I didn't have to walk home again before getting something to eat. I don't remember it myself, but I am told that the Communion breakfast was always hard-boiled eggs and strawberries and cream!

We were now considered to be fully fledged members of the Church and subject to all its laws. One of these decreed that we had to attend Mass every Sunday if at all possible. Failure to do so was a mortal sin. Anyone dying in that parlous state before they had been to Confession went straight to Hell. I have a non-Catholic friend who went to a Catholic Convent School, and she tells me that every Monday morning the nuns there interrogated all the Catholics to find out if there were any backsliders amongst them. Absentees had to have a really cast-iron excuse for staying away or they were given a tongue-lashing they wouldn't forget in a hurry. My friend was extremely thankful to be C. of E.! Nothing as fierce as that happened at St Michael's, but the nuns kept a strict eye on our regular attendance at Mass for all that.

The boys left the Convent at the end of the school year and many of them went on to the Finchley Catholic Grammar School for Boys, as did my brother David in due course. The girls, now officially juniors, left the Villas behind. We came into school by the main entrance, an unimposing door set in the side of the building facing The Grange. It opened in the left-hand corner of a lofty square hall. Several sturdy round pillars outlined an inner square paved with a draughtboard of large black-and-white tiles. A broad strip of matting ran beside the left-hand wall from the entrance door to the opposite side of the hall, where it met the lower corridor at a "T" junction. Halfway along the strip stood the door to the cloakrooms. A wide marble staircase climbed the right-hand wall of the hall, emerging opposite the chapel on the upper corridor. A very large picture of St Michael vanquishing Lucifer hung above it all. It was said to have been painted by one of the school's first pupils and the nuns were justly proud of it.

On our first morning a nun stood at the entrance door and we were taught the first rule of life in the upper school: never walk on the black-and-white tiles of the inner square. Stay on the matting. Anyone caught disobeying this rule would be given a sharp reprimand. Apparently rubber heels made marks on the tiles which were very difficult to get off.

We probably learned our second rule at assembly: the marble staircase was also out of bounds, because the treads were slippery. Only the nuns and lay teachers were allowed to use them. Pupils used the stone staircase at the other end of the building. I occasionally called in to the Convent after I had left and always visited the Chapel. Free from schoolgirl restrictions, I went up by way of the marble staircase, but could never rid myself of the uneasy feeling that a nun would materialise in front of me to administer the dreaded reprimand.

The Grammar School had not yet been built. The Convent School taught all ages in the one building. Even allowing for the additional yearly intake of a number of grant-aided girls, I doubt if there were ever more than 200–250 pupils there at any one time. I don't know how many Sisters lived in the Convent. Their private quarters, known as the Enclosure, were connected to the School by an overhead covered walkway that emerged on the upper corridor through a communicating door next to the Chapel.

This door was always kept locked and each nun had her own key to let herself in and out.

There was no corporal punishment at St Michael's. The upper school equivalent to being stood out at the side of the class was being sent out of the classroom to stand in the corridor. This could be a more severe punishment than it seems at first sight. We always had homework, some of which would be based on a lesson given that day. If that was the lesson the miscreant had missed, having spent the time outside the door, and the homework was not done properly there would be further trouble in store. Not to mention the fact that if Sr Patricia came by and found someone lurking in the corridor during lesson-time there would be an immediate inquisition.

One day part way through the autumn term in 1933, when I was ten years old, I was given a note to take home asking Mother to come and see the Headmistress. I was not aware of being in trouble of any kind, and could not give my mother any clue as to why she had been summoned. It transpired that the English teacher, Miss O'Sullivan, had told Sr Patricia she thought something was amiss with my health. It was suggested that Mother take me to the doctor, which she did. His verdict was a shock. I had outgrown my strength and it was affecting my heart. I must be kept at home to rest until the condition had righted itself. I can only imagine how my parents must have felt. Dismayed and worried, to say the least. My own reaction was one of stupefaction. How had Miss O'Sullivan known? I never found out what she had noticed about me that everyone else, including my parents, had missed. I did not feel ill, only too tired to bother about things sometimes, and assumed that I would only be at home for a few weeks at most; I thought I would be back at school by Christmas. But I was wrong.

4

Senior School: 1934-42

It was the following Easter (1934) before the doctor said I could return to school. But there was a proviso: I must not run about or do anything strenuous. I went back when the summer term began, but could not join in many of the playground games. I was also excluded from netball, tennis and P.E. (Physical Education). And this was not the worst of my troubles. Unfortunately, 1933/34 was the school year in which we started French, Latin, Algebra and Geometry. We had not got beyond the early, simple stages of any of them when I went off sick and during my absence the class had progressed too far for me to catch up. I floundered my way unhappily through the term, and was not surprised when my end-of-year exam results were bad. Even with doing hours of extra homework I was still lagging behind most of the class. I dreaded the thought of going back in the autumn to another term like the last one. It was therefore an immense relief when Sr Patricia told me I would not be going up into the next form in September. She thought it would be better if I stayed down and did the last year over again. And my parents had no choice but to agree.

The prospect of being kept down, which in normal circumstances would have been shameful and embarrassing, seemed to me like an opportunity to make a new beginning. By September, the doctor said, I would be fully fit if I didn't try to do too much during the summer holidays. With Mother keeping a monitoring eye on my every move the whole time, there was little chance of his instructions being allowed to slip my mind. The holidays seemed rather tame as a result, but it was worth it. I set off in September determined to enjoy school life to the full and join in everything going on.

One of the first girls I spoke to in my new class was Mollie. She told me she was C. of E. Her parents had chosen to send her to the Convent because it was an all-girls school and they hoped the nuns would make a lady of her. This she was absolutely determined to resist at every possible opportunity. I admired such independence of spirit enormously and we became firm friends. I might add that the only time I can remember her kicking over the traces and getting caught was when she said "Uh-huh" to one of the nuns instead of "Yes, Sister" and was sent to Sr Patricia for reprimand.

There was a high proportion of non-Catholics at St Michael's. The nuns took great care to avoid any problems that could have arisen from the differences in the C. of E. and R.C. doctrines. Everyone attended Scripture for non-controversial studies of the Bible. Religious Instruction, however, had been taken out of the general curriculum. The Catholics had to be in school twenty minutes early every morning to learn the Catechism and receive instruction in Church dogma before the non-Catholics arrived.

The non-Catholics were always welcome to attend any of our services if they wished to do so. Mollie always came to Benediction (the Blessing) in the Chapel after school on Fridays and, as a member of the school choir, joined us in the gallery for the hymn singing. On the other hand, we Catholics were strictly forbidden to attend the services of any denomination other than our own.

Although the nuns who did the domestic work of the

Convent – the cleaning, cooking, gardening and laundry – were German, like Reverend Mother Herreberga, the teaching nuns were English, with one exception: Sr Mary Fidelis, who taught French, was Viennese. She was not very tall and had a habit of rocking up and down on her toes as she talked. Just before Christmas she put a sprig of fir on each girl's desk with a little white birthday candle attached. It was such a lovely, unexpected thing to do, it took us all by delighted surprise.

Mollie got on very well with Sr Mary Fidelis, who told her one day that she was sure to go to Heaven because she made people laugh. Mollie went home and made herself a white cardboard halo, which she put on with an unnaturally demure expression during the next French lesson. Sr Mary Fidelis bubbled over with laughter when she noticed it.

Because I had a French grandmother and a French Christian name, I think she initially expected me to have a special feeling for the language and become a star pupil. Unfortunately, although I could mimic the accent quite well, I kept forgetting what the words meant, or whether things were masculine or feminine. Having a French grandmother was evidently not sufficient for stardom. A flair for languages would have been better.

In my early years at the school, P.E. was taken by an elderly lady called Miss Wilson. Her exercises were gentle and undemanding. We had no special uniform, doing P.E. in our gym slips. In about 1935 Miss Wilson retired and in came Miss O'Gorman, young and attractive, with new and lively ideas. Suddenly we were doing Swedish drill in divided skirts, no less. It was forbidden, however, to wear French knickers underneath them! I didn't even know what French knickers were. Mollie only knew because her sister-in-law told her. Miss O'Gorman rapidly became a favourite throughout the school. She had lived in India and this seemed to give her certain glamour. If I remember rightly, she injured her back diving off the high board at the swimming pool and was forced to give up gymnastics. I, for one, was utterly heartbroken when she left.

What Sr Mary Bede, the art mistress, thought about this new order of things, I can hardly imagine. She was an extremely genteel person, very easily shocked. In my first memory of her, she is sitting with bowed head, her hand over her eyes. It was a day of school entertainments – probably St Michael's Feast Day. One of the classes was giving a display of Irish jigs, or the Highland fling, or some other energetic dance. Their skirts were flying up, showing their regulation navy blues, and Sr Mary Bede could not bear the sight of such indecency. Rumour said she had been Lady Somebody before she became a nun and it may well have been true. Moira Lympany, the concert pianist, was known to be her niece and Miss Lympany did have aristocratic connections. Besides her official role as art teacher, Sr Mary Bede took an unofficial interest in other aspects of our education: the correct use of the English language at all times and the promotion of good handwriting, to name but two. I don't think I quite appreciated this when, at the age of about twelve, I happened to tell her I was writing a short story. She said she would like to read what I had done so far and invited me to bring it along the following Saturday morning. Although I was of course flattered by her interest, I was not entirely happy about it. At one point in the story a boy and a girl had to swap clothes behind a bush. Something to do with fooling the villains, I think – it was that sort of story. Knowing her prim and proper outlook, I was uneasy about her reaction to this bit of the plot. However, she read the whole thing through without comment and I thought all was well. Then she got out her red pen and took my story apart word by word, until the pages were littered with her suggested alterations and corrections. She also criticised my handwriting. I can't recall ever finishing that story. If I did, I certainly never went back to Sr Mary Bede with it.

Our art teacher's style of painting was minutely detailed and every detail had to be accurate. I remember labouring over a pink hyacinth, putting in one floret at a time until I was sick of the sight of it. Which is not to say we found her lessons boring: usually I enjoyed them, but not always for the right reason. On the whole art was looked on as a period of relaxation between other more important subjects. Sr Mary Bede was a much better artist than she was disciplinarian and there were times when our chatter tried her patience to its limits. She would raise her voice above the hubbub and plead, "*Please* don't make so much noise, girls. You're giving me an awful headache." And, wretches that we were, we thought this was funny and sniggered behind our hands!

Sr Mary Bede also involved herself in the stage productions put on by the school each year. Every form took part in these at one time or another. The Infants presented the Christmas Nativity Play; the older girls, directed by Miss O'Sullivan, who taught English and Literature, tackled anything from modern-day sketches to excerpts from Shakespeare. Whatever it was, the cast always did their best to provide their own costumes if possible. Anything that could not be brought from home had to be supplied from the school's collection of stage clothes held by Sr Mary Bede. From a large box filled with the remnants of past productions she would pull out lengths of material, pieces of gauze, shawls or gaudy scarves and drape them over and around the players until she had the effect she wanted. Useless to protest "It's got a hole in it, Sister," or "It's all crumpled." "It won't show when you're up on the stage," she would assure us firmly. "The creases will drop out. No one will notice." There was nothing for it but to hope she was right.

Another event with which I associate Sr Mary Bede was the annual Summer Fete. Not so much the fete itself, but the preparations for it. During the preceding week local shops and organisations sympathetic to the school donated various items suitable for raffle and competition prizes. A friendly chemist donated a quantity of bath cubes, cakes of scented soap, sachets of shampoo and the like. Artistically arranged in small boxes covered with fancy paper and decorated with ribbon, they made an attractive display on the Gift Stall. Making up the boxes was a task undertaken jointly by Sr Mary Bede and, under her guidance, a working-party of seniors. Our boxes rarely looked as good as hers, but nevertheless they were quite presentable.

The school's great ambition for the fete was to make a net profit of £100, a distant target that we all strained to achieve. Every girl was expected to sell as many admission programmes as possible before the event. Relatives and family friends and neighbours were all pestered into buying programmes whether they were coming to the fete or not. In addition we were sent out in pairs to try our luck at door-to-door selling in the street surrounding the school. Some people were sharp verging on rude when they heard our mission, others said, "No, thank you" with a pleasant smile. A few actually bought a programme. The girl who raised the most money earned special points for her House and competition to be the winner was fierce. We had never heard the term "hard sell", but some of the girls were very good at it.

Our other contribution to the day's success was to pray, collectively in Assembly and privately in our morning and evening prayers: "Please, please God, don't let it rain on Saturday!"

The fete was held on the big lawn. It was very much a family affair. Most of the sideshows were home-made. Father made and ran one of them. A circular wooden board about three feet across was brightly painted in segments of different colours and widths. A large pointer swung round in the centre. I think it was one (old) penny a go to give it a twirl. If it stopped on one particular colour the player won sixpence (two and a half pence). This didn't happen often. The sixpenny segment was very narrow. One of the most popular attractions was the round tower mat slide. It looked death-defying but it probably wasn't as high as it looked then.

There was always a lot of excited running up and down the long lime walk between the fete and the school during the afternoon. And not only by the girls. My brother David said that when he was about eleven, he and a gang of cronies were having a high old time chasing girls round the pillars in the entrance hall. Suddenly a tall, angry nun descended on them out of nowhere, like the wrath of God, ordering them out in no uncertain terms. David and the cronies fled in panic, leaving the girls to fend for themselves. I suspect that the nun (Sr Patricia?) was even more angry at the marks their shoes were making on the black and white tiles than she was about the horseplay itself.

Mollie lived about as far from the school in a southerly direction as I did to the north. Neither of us had to be in until teatime at five o'clock and I often walked home with her. She would then about turn and walk halfway back with me, both of us talking non-stop. Her father was as strict as mine and as we grew older we spent much time bemoaning their restrictions, particularly the one that forbade us to have boyfriends while we were still at school. I felt especially aggrieved about this, not to say deprived. Mollie had two older brothers and she at least got a chance to talk to some of their friends occasionally. My brother, being four years younger than I, was no help socially at all. All his friends were too young for me to be interested in them. As far as I was concerned older boys might just as well have been creatures from outer space. The only friendship I ever made with a boy of my own age lasted for most of one

Saturday afternoon. I was about twelve at the time. I have forgotten his name and can hardly recall what he looked like, but I do remember the two of us chasing the baker's van, now motorised, up Mayfield Avenue. It was going slowly and the tailboard was down as the baker had not finished his round. Catching up, we scrambled onto the tailboard. When the van stopped we slid off before the driver could get to the back to refill his basket. While he dealt with his next customer, we stowaways kept out of sight. When he climbed back into the driving seat we sprinted for the tailboard and clung on tight until the van stopped again. We did this several times without getting caught. It was great fun and we saw no danger in our game.

We expected the driver to continue his round all the way up Mayfield Avenue to the High Road, but he didn't. He turned into Linton Avenue, the short link road between Mayfield and Finchley Park, and he speeded up! Clinging on for dear life, I hardly had time to be frightened before he reached the end of Linton Avenue and turned left into Finchley Park. Then I really did get scared. If the van didn't stop soon we would be going past our house. It did stop, but we were not quite quick enough gathering our wits. The baker saw us sliding to the ground and swore, horror-struck. "Wot the bleedin' 'ell?" I started to giggle with nerves and relief. He turned on me in anger. "Stupid kids! Yer could 'ave been killed." He raised his fist and shouted, "Clear orf! Go on, clear orf!"

I glanced up the road and stopped laughing. Ignoring the baker, the boy grabbed my hand to pull me back to Linton Avenue. "Come on. We can go up Mayfield."

"I can't," I jerked my head towards the tall figure striding purposefully down the road towards us. "That's my father."

"Cripes!" The boy let go my hand and began to run. At the corner of Linton Avenue he paused to call back, "I'll look out for you in the Park. OK?"

Taking in the situation, the baker began refilling his basket for his next customers, still berating me. "Now yer'll be for it. Serves yer right! Young fools!" I left him and started up the road to meet my father.

We walked back to the house in silence. I had been wondering how he had spotted us. The garden fork stuck into the soil by the front gate gave me my answer. The baker's shout had doubtless made him look up, and there we were – caught in the act. Mother came out of the kitchen and looked from Father's face to mine and back again. "What's wrong?" she demanded. "What happened?"

"Tell your mother what you were doing," ordered Father curtly.

It was only as I described our game that I realised it had indeed been dangerous. The baker was right, we could have been killed. Or at least injured. I said, "I'm sorry, Mummy," and meant it.

I can't recall the whole of the conversation. I know I was forbidden to go out unless it was with my usual friends. The words that really stuck in my mind were Father's: "I forbid you to see or speak to that boy again. Do you understand?" In those days fathers tended to be far more heavy handed than they are today.

Our home life was run to a strict routine. Tea was at five o'clock. If I spent too much time after school walking backwards and forwards with Mollie and came in late, I was in trouble. I don't think it happened very often because if I was late I missed the beginning of *Children's Hour* on the wireless. I loved that programme, especially the plays. At six o'clock the wireless was switched off and the evening given over to homework. In addition to the two – sometimes three – subjects set for the whole class each evening, the Catholics had to memorise the answers to a given number of Catechism questions, ready for Religious Instruction the following morning. By the time I had finished my homework it was nearly time for bed. I had had my hour of freedom before tea and was not normally allowed out in the evenings in term-time.

David and I were very different in our attitudes towards our work. He actually enjoyed homework! He got down to it as soon as he got in from school and therefore had his evenings relatively free. Usually he disappeared to do something with the Cubs or, later, the Scouts. Whatever it was I don't remember him being home much in the evenings.

At that time R.C. children were confirmed at the age of eleven or twelve, rather earlier than the C. of E. children. The ceremony is performed by the Bishop of the diocese, which in itself made the day important. My memory of the event is hazy. I remember the altar seemed crowded with priests and altar servers attending the Bishop. And I think the choir was singing as we knelt before the Bishop one by one to kiss the Episcopal ring on the hand he extended towards us. The kiss was our pledge of allegiance. He then made the sign of the cross with holy oil on our foreheads. We were now officially Soldiers of Christ.

When it was Mollie's turn, a couple of years later, I found myself in a dilemma. We were, as I have said, forbidden to enter any other church but our own. To attend a service in a C. of E. church was unthinkable. I conferred with another friend, also a Catholic, who wanted to attend. After giving the matter serious thought we decided that Confirmations were social occasions, like weddings. People went to watch, not to take part. So we went along and sat at the back of the church. We stood up and knelt down when everyone else did and, purely out of courtesy, bowed our heads during the prayers. But we did not pray. And we kept very quiet about it at school afterwards.

The official school leaving age was fourteen. Several girls left to attend commercial colleges or go out to work. Those of us who stayed on to take our School Leaving Certificate began to feel too old to be treated like children. We were growing up, and tried to think of ways to assert our individuality. Not an easy thing to do. No jewellery or personal adornment was permitted other than a cross or holy medals on a chain. (Though come to think of it, I can recall being allowed to wear a little gold signet ring given to me by Nannie and Aunty Evelyn for my fourteenth birthday.) Make-up was out of the question. A girl who took dancing lessons turned up at one of the summer fetes wearing lipstick and was viewed with horror as a scarlet woman. Not that some of us had more than a hazy idea what a scarlet woman actually did. What with that and the dancing we were troubled by fear that she would never be allowed into Heaven.

Some brave spirits put tucks round the crown of their velour hat, just above the brim. This got rid of the hated 'po' effect and allowed the hat to be worn at a jaunty angle, but Sr Patricia soon put a stop to that. Vanity was not to be encouraged.

We were also forbidden to curl our hair. When the pageboy hairstyle came into fashion Mollie devised a method of reproducing it without actually using curlers. You dampened the ends of your hair before leaving home in the morning and turned it under, pinning it round a thick strand of cotton wool. Your hat held it in place to dry on the way to school, where the hair grips and cotton wool were surreptitiously removed in the cloakroom. The hair combed out into a very good, natural-looking pageboy that would stay in place all day – unless it rained. But there was trouble if you were caught. I got caught by my mother before I even left the house. From then on, despite my wailing protests, my father, who cut our hair, kept mine too short to tuck round the cotton wool. And my mother approved. She may not have agreed with the accepted attitude of the day on sex education, but she was no freethinker when it came to school discipline.

One of the seniors, a girl with naturally straight hair of no particular colour, turned up one Monday morning with bright curly hair, obviously bleached and permed. When she took her hat off in the cloakroom there was a sharp intake of breath from those nearest her, a moment of nudging and murmuring as the word went round, then a buzz of eager anticipation. What would Sr Patricia do when she saw her? What Sr Patricia did was to fetch a hairbrush, march the girl off to the toilets, hold her head down in one of the washbasins and brush her hair vigorously under the cold tap. Having towelled it roughly dry she made the poor girl stand up on the stage during Assembly, to face the whole school with her hair in a damp frizz. A warning and deterrent to anyone who might be tempted to follow her example. And it worked. Mollie gave up her trick with the cotton wool and the hair grips. Until the fuss had died down, anyway. I believe the girl left soon after this episode. It was whispered that she had been expelled, but I think it is more likely that she left by mutual agreement between her parents and Sr Patricia.

The nuns had lost some of their mystique as we grew older. Even Sr Patricia, though she never lost our respect and obedience. She was strict but fair and to my knowledge she never had favourites.

1934/35 was the school year in which the form was divided into two halves: one taking Latin, the other science. For some reason which I never understood, I was put in the Latin half. I had even less feeling for Latin than I had for French. Sr Teresa Alfonso, the Latin mistress, ("T.A." behind her back) was extremely patient, and I did work at it, the second time around, but it was always hard going. Mollie was doing science and I envied her.

In 1937 or 38 Sr Mary Bede retired from teaching. Her place was taken by a young nun with totally different ideas and methods to the ones we were accustomed to. Sr Mary Emelda did not put up objects on a stand for us to copy, as

Sr Mary Bede had done. She gave us a theme and left us to interpret it for ourselves. Gone were the carefully drawn outlines, the meticulous details and the intricately decorated borders. Sr Mary Emelda liked broad scenes covering the whole paper. "Use plenty of paint," she would say. "Don't be afraid of it." The results were sometimes unpredictable. 1938 was a year of political tension. The air was full of rumour and talk of another war. Public air-raid shelters were being built in the streets and trenches dug in open spaces, giving people a chance to take cover if they were caught out in an air raid. So the topical theme for one particular art lesson was "Digging Trenches in The Park". Following instructions I filled my brush with browns and greens for the earth and grass and plastered colour liberally over the paper until it buckled under the onslaught. Pools of greenish brown sludge began to form, until the whole thing looked more like the bottom of a dirty pond than somewhere offering escape from flying shrapnel.

In my last year at school I was made House Prefect. I was not really comfortable in the job. A part of my duties was to tour the classrooms every week, as already mentioned, to monitor the performance of the Blues in each form. My visits took place after school and the girls could not leave until I had finished saying whatever I thought needed saying. As I reproved girls for doing – or not doing – all the things I myself had been reproved for in the not too distant past, I felt like an impostor masquerading as a Prefect. Had my predecessors felt the same? If so, they had never shown it and I did my best to follow their example. I had to say my piece quickly because, having stayed in the classroom to await my arrival, the girls were all anxious to be off home, edging for the door if I went on too long.

It should have been a happy time for me, knowing that the petty rules and restrictions I had been mentally kicking against for months were coming to an end. Freedom beckoned. But life was overshadowed by a monumental row I had caused at home. My father had always had his mind set on my going into the Civil Service because it would be a safe job for life. I hated the idea. I wanted to work with people not, as I saw it, be buried alive filling in endless forms in triplicate for evermore. To escape such a fate I had deliberately failed to put my name down for the Civil Service entrance exam. Worse, I had kept Father in ignorance of what I had done – or in this case not done – until the last date for application had safely passed and it was too late for him to do anything about it. The repercussions when he found out rumbled on for weeks. So great was Father's disappointment that he could not bring himself to speak to me; the atmosphere in the house was so unhappy that it started to affect my schoolwork. My homework was badly done and I could not concentrate in class. The deterioration in my work was soon brought to the attention of the Headmistress.

Sr Patricia, strict and awe-inspiring as she was, had a surprisingly sympathetic ear for any girl who appeared to be grappling with a problem she couldn't deal with. She took me for a walk in the grounds and under her gentle questioning I eventually told her the whole story. There was nothing she could do about the Civil Service, but she did talk me into a less rebellious frame of mind. I agreed to stay at school for a further year to take the commercial course, which I had stubbornly refused to consider when Father suggested it. "Your parents are quite right," said Sr Patricia, "shorthand and typing will stand you in good stead for whatever you want to do later."

Mollie and I left school in July 1939. We had been happy there and on the day we broke up our joy at the prospect of freedom from the restrictions of school, homework and exams was slightly marred by regret that we would be splitting up to go our separate ways. Any illusions we – or was it only I? – might have cherished that once away from school the world would be ours for the taking, died quickly in the face of reality. The outbreak of the Second World War in the September changed everything. Mollie ended up in a top-secret Government Department working in one of the endless miles of tunnels that ran beneath Whitehall. I returned to school as agreed.

I found the place much changed. All the pupils, together with the nuns and lay teachers, had been evacuated to the country for safety. An almost eerie silence hung over the empty school building. The commercial course was being held in one of the old villas. Our classroom had been the cloakroom in my infant school days. But some things had not altered. We had homework, exams, rules and regulations exactly as before. Only the content of the lessons was different. And at home, although an uneasy peace existed between me and my father, I was still not allowed out in the evenings, this time because of the blackout!

As for the commercial course itself, I was good at shorthand, but failed every typing test because I was too slow. If I tried to speed up I made mistakes. The instructress assured me it was just a matter of practice. If I persevered, my fingers would automatically speed up. I left St Michael's in 1940 with a Pitman's Shorthand Certificate for 120 words per minute to add to my School Leaving Certificate, and a sincere hope that my typing really would improve of its own accord when I was actually working.

My first job was junior shorthand/typist in the welfare office of a hospital. My typing, as predicted, did improve and I was happy.

However, as the war intensified, more and more men were needed in the Forces. Large numbers were conscripted and it was rumoured that women and girls were also going to be called up to free some of the men for 'active service'. Father, still determined to keep me safe, organised a

Yvonne, 1939

shorthand typing job for me in an Income Tax collection office. (The Civil Service was exempt from conscription.) He also arranged an interview for me to take the formal entrance test, taking it for granted that I would pass. With bitter resentment and shaky confidence I did as I was told and presented myself at the appointed time. The Collector, obviously hostile, picked up his morning *Times* and dictated one of the leaders at a speed far greater than my modest capability. Even if the subject had not been Japanese foreign policy, I would not have been able to keep up with him. As for typing it back, I never got that far. I admitted defeat and left in tears, my confidence in rags.

Despite the disastrous interview, I had already been given the job behind the scenes and I had to take it. Hating every minute I was in the place, I worked there until I discovered that I could escape by volunteering for one of the Services. I chose the Air Force, joining the WAAF, the Women's Auxiliary Air Force, in 1942.

But that is another story. (See *"Have You Got Your Irons?" It's a Waaf's Life*.)

Part Two: David's Story

5

Finchley: 1927-44

I was born on 28 March 1927, two years after my parents moved into a new terraced house in North Finchley. I joined my sister Yvonne, who was four years old. It was a fairly comfortable house by early 1920s standards. Father was a Civil Servant working as a supervisor in the printing section of His Majesty's Stationery Office, so he was relatively well paid. Money, however, was tight. Mother had a lot of ill health and needed treatment, which had to be paid for in those pre-National Health Service days. Also I was a sickly child, suffering from several ailments which incurred further expense. One of these was acidosis. I had to chew charcoal biscuits to aid my digestion. They looked and tasted like black dog biscuits. I much preferred the spoonful of Virol – a thick sweet extract of malt – that I had to take every day. In addition, everything possible was sprinkled with Glucodin which, as the name implies, was based on glucose.

This regime continued for some years and the combination of sweet things not only rotted my teeth but gave me a taste for sweet stuff that I had great difficulty in outgrowing in later life.

My memories of the first five years are slight, but I vividly remember the excitement of the whole family listening to the early broadcasts of the BBC, which had recently been renamed from 2LO, on a cat's whisker radio built by Father. The apparatus was set up in the front sitting room and we listened through headphones. Loudspeakers came later and were considered to be of poor design.

I also remember a pokerwork sign that hung on the kitchen wall behind the table: "No talking during mealtimes". It hung there for several years until I managed to get it down and Yvonne threw it over the garden fence to land behind our neighbour's shed. When questioned about its disappearance we both stoutly denied all knowledge of it. I doubt if we were believed, but I cannot recollect either of our parents pursuing the subject. Perhaps they realised the sign had had its day.

When I reached school age, due to the fact that I was not very strong, and because of Father's financial position – by this time Yvonne was at a fee-paying convent school – I was sent to St John's Primary School in Britannia Road, just around the corner from Finchley Park. I was, I think, the only Catholic in the school and was bullied unmercifully and sometimes physically assaulted by the other pupils. The girls were as bad as the boys. Obviously the situation could not continue, especially as the staff appeared to turn a blind eye to what was going on, despite complaints by my parents. So after a few months I was moved to St Michael's Convent in Nether Street where my sister was already a pupil. The Convent took boys between the ages of five and eight, at which point they had to move on to another school. Mixed-sex education in convents was still a long way in the future. My days there were fairly forgettable except that the nuns who took us for lessons were very kind in view of the problems I had experienced at St John's. I could not believe my good fortune in the change of school.

In 1935, at the age of eight, I moved on to the Finchley Catholic Grammar School in Woodside Road about three-quarters of a mile away. It had been established in the late

1920s by Father Parsons, parish priest of St Alban's Catholic Church in Nether Street, opposite St Michael's Convent. He used to maintain that the standard of education matched that of certain public schools of that time. A claim difficult to prove or disprove. There appeared to be no scholarship system in operation so I was a fee-paying pupil. Fortunately at about this time Father was promoted to Superintendent of Somerset House and was able to find the additional money to pay for me. Moving to an all-boys school from a convent was quite a change of direction. I now began to learn to a set curriculum. I enjoyed the schoolwork and, later, the homework.

Being an all-boys school, the discipline was quite strict. Corporal punishment, unknown at St Michael's, was administered by either Father Parsons or Mr Metcalfe, the Deputy Head. They did not use a cane, they used what was known as the "tolly", a fearsome weapon comprising a leather tongue about the size of an adult shoe sole attached to a short wooden handle. This was applied to the hands for normal offences or to the bottom for really serious crimes. I only remember the latter occurring once during my time at the school. A pupil being questioned about a suspected forged sick letter hit the Deputy Head. For this he received a public beating and was then expelled. I found the spectacle degrading to watch and felt ashamed on his behalf. Which is more than I felt when I myself got "six of the best" on my hands for the first time. On the contrary, despite the pain, I felt proud. Newcomers were not really accepted as 'one of us' until they had had at least one leathering.

Father Parsons, who was later made a Monsignor, was a Jekyll and Hyde personality. He was a brilliant headmaster, having a total understanding of boys. Although strict he was very fair and all the pupils respected him. In the pulpit on a Sunday morning, however, he was a transformed character who forcibly expressed his views on everything from the religious obligations of his flock to politics and how they should vote in elections. He bullied his captive audience in a way which would not now be accepted by the laity. He was ultra right wing in his views, openly supporting Franco in the Spanish Civil War of 1936 to 1938. He denounced the Government forces as Communists, atheists and Russian puppets. One year, when I was about twelve, I was awarded as form prize a book called *I Found No Peace* by a journalist who had covered the war from Franco's side. A very disturbing book, and totally biased. It was not until some years later that I came to recognise that excesses and religious persecution had been carried out by both sides and that the war was used as a proving ground for new weapons by both Russia and Germany.

Because I was still not very strong I was not allowed to play football, which was a compulsory subject. As this was played on a Saturday morning I had more freedom than other pupils and started to develop an interest in walking. There were several parks and open spaces in the immediate neighbourhood, such as Friary Park, and I would wander off alone to explore them. There was no worry expressed by my parents for doing something that in these days would be considered "at risk". One eagerly pursued activity, which I thoroughly enjoyed, was a regular clash between the pupils of my old school St John's and our school. These took place at a small recreation ground just off Woodside Road called The Roughlocks, now upgraded to the Swan Lane Open Space. It was a wonderful place for youngsters, having a pond, lots of shrubbery, banks to be climbed and a small wood. These meetings got very physical at times and it was quite normal to get back home muddy and exhausted but with a feeling of great satisfaction at having met and done battle with the enemy who had given me so much grief in the past. How these meetings were arranged I am not certain but news of an impending coming together would be passed around and troops mustered.

By the time I was about ten I was much stronger and had started playing sports, which included football, cricket (which I loathed) and tennis. I was pretty useless at all of them, being both left-handed and lacking the degree of coordination necessary to succeed. However, I enjoyed tennis and played it a lot. My sports master's comment on one end-of-term report stated: "David plays sport with more enthusiasm than skill", and this really says it all! I had also taken up cycling and by the time I was twelve I used to cycle miles out into the countryside north of London, always on my own. I had three very good school friends but we did little together after school mainly because we all lived in different directions to one another. I had also joined the Boy Scouts, so I had very little spare time.

September 1939 changed the lives of everybody, and mine was no exception. The family was about to go on holiday to Swanage in August when Father's leave was suddenly cancelled and he received instructions to attend briefings on what would happen in the event of war being declared. Plans were in place to move essential Government departments out of London. A number of them, including Father's, were to be evacuated to Llandudno in North Wales. One consequence of Father's move was that during what transpired to be a momentous period in history Mother ran the home in Finchley on her own. I can't remember her going to Llandudno at any time or Father coming home on leave, though he probably did. Mother spent the war years working at the Citizens' Advice Bureau at Tally Ho! Corner and I think she enjoyed the work and involvement.

Being active in the Scouts led me in 1940 to volunteer to become a messenger attached to the local ARP Unit, which had its headquarters underneath the Odeon cinema in the High Street. My function when on duty was to relay messages, cycling between the ARP posts in the Finchley area. I also attended incidents with the wardens and heavy rescue crews. Although North Finchley escaped fairly lightly during the Blitz, we did have our share of bombs and incendiaries and one land mine. Later in the war a number of V1 doodlebugs also came down in the neigbourhood. My overall general memory of the Blitz was the drone of German bombers with the searchlight fingers trying to pick them up and illuminate them for the anti-aircraft guns to shoot down. We had ack-ack guns sited on the golf course at the end of our road, and mobile guns were parked along the A1. We never ever saw or heard any air activity by our own fighters.

Two incidents stand out in my memory. The first involved a stick of bombs that were dropped along the A1, now the A1000 High Street. One sliced a house in half in Highwood Avenue, about three hundred yards from where we lived. The ARP services, including myself, attended the incident and found that a young girl had been stranded unharmed on the first floor. She could not get down as the door of the room was part of the wall that had been demolished. Her rescue was carried out fairly quickly by her mother and the ARP services who got her out onto the outhouse roof.

Many years later, talking with my sister Yvonne I discovered that she was still in touch with the young girl, whose name is Denise Hannigan. Denise recalls that although she was physically unharmed in the incident, the traumatic effect on her was considerable. It affected her schoolwork so badly that she had to stay down and do that year over again.

It is interesting to look back and remember that very close to the bombed house was one used by the Scouts to store items they had collected locally for recycling. If this house had been hit it would have burned like a tinderbox as all the rooms were full of, among other things, newspapers, cardboard and books. Even at the time we used to wonder why the nearby residents did not complain, but in those days people had a different view of things. They probably saw it as helping the war effort.

The second incident involved a land mine. This was a large-calibre bomb dropped by parachute, usually exploding while still airborne. This one fell at New Southgate, about two miles away from North Finchley, and caused massive damage and a large number of casualties. It was out of our area, but our group was called in because of the size of the incident. As a thirteen-year-old I was affected deeply by the amount of destruction I witnessed.

My scouting activities continued throughout the war. I joined a C. of E. troop based at St Barnabas Church, Woodside Avenue and became friendly with Terry Malone, the only other Catholic in the troop. He was a year older than myself and went to St Ignatius School in London. We needed mutual support because at that time there was a certain amount of religious intolerance in the group. We were given a hard time by some of the older Scouts. We treated this attitude with the contempt it deserved and eventually both of us became patrol leaders and King's Scouts. Our main outdoor activities included collecting aluminium and waste paper for recycling, as previously mentioned. For light relief we had occasional scouting camps at either Mill Hill or slightly further afield. Later we installed Morrison indoor air-raid shelters. These were made of very heavy metal sheets and uprights and were erected in ground-floor rooms. It was hard work heaving all the material around but we enjoyed the job and our troop was responsible for erecting a large number in the Finchley area. One house we called at to install a shelter had a spiked metal chain along the pathway leading to the front door. I pressed the bell, stepped back and fell over the chain. I received a gash from the back of my knee to the top of my leg which required immediate medical attention as I was bleeding profusely. I was taken to the Finchley Memorial Hospital where I had about twenty stitches inserted without anaesthetic. In those days Boy Scouts were obviously considered to be either stoics or expendable. I managed to persuade my mother to have a shelter installed but she never used it. Her reaction to the bombing was phlegmatic. She had experienced it before, during the 1914–18 war, and her attitude was a great example to me, as I often felt scared, particularly when on duty with the ARP during air raids.

Yvonne and I got on very well together from an early age. However, the age gap of four years meant that to some extent we tended to go our own ways. When I started at St Michael's Convent she played her part in ferrying me to and fro, which she probably found a bit restricting. I don't think we ever had a major fall out. The worst incident I can remember occurred on a Sunday morning trip to church. Yvonne could be a bit of a tease and I was never smart enough to be able to respond with a suitable answer. Just as we were walking into church she made a comment which really upset me, so in frustration I hit her on top of her hat with my fist. Unfortunately I was seen by a sidesman who promptly told Father who had already entered the church, and the result was that I was in disgrace. Not necessarily for hitting my sister, which was bad enough, but for doing it in the house of God. I was sent to my room and cannot remember whether I was also caned. The worst punishment was getting no food for the rest of the day.

By the time I started extending my social activities at the age of sixteen Yvonne had already been in the WAAF a year. She only came to one of our Saturday night dances at the Red Lion, Barnet, and probably thought we were a bit juvenile. The only person in the gang she really knew was Terry Malone.

During the spring of 1941 I was out on one of my solo

cycle rides in Potters Bar, about fifteen miles from home, when I suddenly felt an acute pain in my stomach. I struggled back home, arriving in a state of near collapse. Mother promptly called the doctor, who diagnosed acute appendicitis necessitating immediate surgery. I was taken by ambulance to the Colney Hatch Hospital, which pre-war had been a secure mental asylum. All the bed patients had been evacuated and the establishment turned into a general hospital at the outbreak of the war. The only patients left were the very severe cases confined to individual rooms or cells underground. I vividly remember being wheeled to theatre on a trolley down a long corridor and seeing the inmates staring out of the securely guarded windows in the doors. Some were shouting and screaming, others were entirely placid. It was like a scene from Dante's *Inferno*. Whilst I was there we had a very noisy air raid, and a bomb dropped in the hospital grounds. Those patients who were mobile dived under their beds, by which time windows were falling in. Luckily no one was seriously hurt.

At sixteen, with good exam results behind me I was in a dilemma as to which career path to follow. I was very keen to get into the services so I volunteered for the Fleet Air Arm to become a pilot. One of the reasons for choosing this branch of the services was so that I could join up at seventeen and a quarter, whereas the Navy's earliest age, apart from boy entry, was seventeen and a half. I passed the initial educational exams and medical some time in 1943, and was told I would be called up as near to seventeen and a quarter as was viable, depending upon the timing of initial training courses. I officially became a CW (Commission Warrant) candidate. This was equivalent to an officer cadet in the army.

On the recommendation of my school and the urging of Father I joined an old-established firm of City chartered accountants located in Ludgate Hill in the shadow of St

David and Yvonne

Paul's Cathedral. I was accepted on three months' probation with a view to signing articles to become a chartered accountant. I knew on the very first day that I had made a mistake. I hated the work, and although I got out a number of times to audit the clients' books, I could not wait for my probation period to be completed. The final decision was taken out of my hands a few weeks after starting. Another probationer, also from my school, and I used to creep into the manager's office during the lunch hour when he was absent. He had a wonderful collection of African trophies on the walls, including spears and shields, and we would take them off the wall and play war games. Unfortunately, one day he came back to his office early and caught us red-handed. At our subsequent interview with him he was quite nice about the incident, but suggested that I should consider a career move – a view with which I heartily agreed – and was given a month's notice.

Father was mortified when I told him but I got another position quite quickly. At that time movement of labour was strictly controlled so I had to sign on at the local Labour

Exchange which I thought at that time was very demeaning. In actual fact the staff were extremely helpful and put me forward for a vacancy as a laboratory assistant at the Mill Hill gasworks, an easy cycle ride from home. After a fairly stiff interview I started work a couple of weeks later. The work itself turned out to be very interesting. The laboratory was responsible for routine testing of the coal furnace temperatures, gas sampling, analysing of by-products such as tar oil and benzene, and the gas filter beds. This last operation involved digging out samples from the earth beds for analysis. The smell of gas permeated everything. It got into my clothes which when washed would give off a very strong odour. It was not a social occupation. The benzene was stored in a large tank about 30 feet high and it was necessary to climb up an outside ladder, open a manhole, and drop a sample bottle and dipstick into the tank. As soon as the manhole was opened heavy vapour fumes would be released which could cause dizziness if inhaled. Although I had been warned about this I was not told for some time that my predecessor had been overcome by the fumes and had fallen into the tank and died. As the tank held several thousand gallons, emptying it to remove his body must have been a very difficult job. I wonder what the present day Health and Safety Executive would say about this? Certainly safety did not appear to rate very highly in those days. The tar oil was pumped into rail tankers and again it was necessary to sample by climbing on top of the tanker and opening a hatch. It was awful stuff to handle, and even though I wore protective clothing it got over everything.

All testing was done in a large well-equipped laboratory. There were only three other staff: a manager, a female senior chemist and another older laboratory assistant. They were all very pleasant people, and I was encouraged to enrol for a two-year Inter-BSc Course. The academic level was pitched somewhere between the present-day A level and

BSc. I signed up at the Northern Polytechnic, Holloway, to take physics, chemistry and botany three nights a week. In addition there was a lot of homework to be done across the other four days of the week. It was very hard going, but I was allowed to leave early to get home, change, and then take public transport comprising trolleybus and trams to Holloway. I started the course in September 1943 and completed the first year by June 1944. Knowing that all things being well I would probably join up in the July, there was no way in which I could complete the second year without applying for exemption from the services. I decided that the second year could wait until after the war was over.

All this activity was happening at a time when, liberated from school, I had started to sample life. Terry Malone introduced me to a number of his friends from St Ignatius and other grammar schools in the Finchley area. We formed a loose gang which included a few girls, in particular Margery Evamy and Elizabeth Knowles-Brown. It was an unspoken understanding that we did not pair off with the girls. If we did it would be severely frowned upon. Lapses did occur, and I had a soft spot for Elizabeth, but never tried to date her. My first introduction to the opposite sex had occurred when I was about fifteen. I had a crush on a girl called Eileen O'Connor who lived in Nether Street and whose father was choirmaster at St Albans. I followed her home a couple of times after Mass on Sunday at a discreet distance, but was too nervous to speak to her. The third time she got fed up with my antics and asked if I wanted to walk home with her. As this was only a few hundred yards from the church we did not have a great deal of time to say much, except for me to ask her to a dance at St Bartholomew's Church hall. I had been taking dancing lessons and my teacher said I had great potential, a statement which she did not qualify and was somewhat ambiguous. I therefore felt pretty confident that I could put up a reasonable showing.

However, the evening was a complete disaster, Eileen actually going home with somebody else. The trouble was that I suffered dreadfully from shyness and could not produce the required small talk on the first date.

Our crowd used to meet up every Saturday evening and walk either to the Red Lion at High Barnet, a distance of about four miles, or more often to the Cherry Tree at Totteridge and there we would get pleasantly mellow on cider or weak beer, and occasionally go to a dance in the school hall next to the pub. We got a reputation for being high-spirited and at times a bit noisy. The village bobby used to keep an eye on us at these functions and viewed us with great suspicion. On one notable occasion he followed us from the pub to the hall where, having been refused entry because we were fooling about, we gatecrashed the dance. The police officer appeared and ordered us off the premises, following us out into the dark to see what we got up to outside. One of our party hid behind a wall, and as he walked past knocked his helmet off with a long piece of wood, leaving him to search around for his missing headgear. That was our worst incident, but we also regularly moved road signs, on one occasion carrying a temporary No Entry sign all the way back to Tally Ho! Corner, where we left it outside a shop whose owner we did not care for. It was scandalous behaviour for teenagers, but we never did any real damage or became involved in brawls. We used to walk miles, and often got home very late. I had a rule: never to go home under the influence. This sometimes meant walking round the block a number of times to sober up before creeping into the house without waking Mother. As far as I know, she never twigged what we got up to, but if she did she never raised the issue with me.

At the end of 1943 Father, who was still at Llandudno, was diagnosed as having TB, believed to have been caused by the terrible conditions he experienced in the trenches during the Great War. He was going to be transferred back to Finchley for home nursing, and arrangements were made to accommodate him downstairs. Yvonne applied for compassionate leave from the WAAF to help Mother nurse him, and this was granted. At this point Father was accepted as an in-patient at a TB sanatorium, Clare Hall, South Mimms in Middlesex, and he started his two-year programme of treatment in February 1944. Father's move to Clare Hall made it possible for both Mother and Yvonne to visit him during the week. In those days the treatment for TB was to collapse the lung, if only one was affected, and keep the patient outdoors in all weathers on an open veranda. It was literally a kill or cure approach and Father, who was in his mid forties, was very fortunate to be selected. Anyone of his age was usually written off to die naturally. A number of inmates were service people in their twenties and the man in the next bed to Father was an RAF air crew member whose plane had ditched in the sea. He had suffered serious exposure before being rescued, and as a consequence had contracted TB. He was a very nice lad but sadly he did not recover.

As Clare Hall was within easy cycling distance I used to visit Father at weekends. I have to admit to finding the atmosphere depressing. So many young men through no fault of their own were having to fight to survive. It was typical of Father that he adopted a very positive approach to his illness and used to do a lot of leather work, producing beautifully hand-stitched bags, wallets and writing cases, one of which I still have.

At seventeen I decided to join the Home Guard and learn the basics of military training before joining up. I was attached to the unit at Whetstone and was immensely proud of my uniform and rifle. We paraded once a week and at weekends had rifle practice at the Mill Hill barracks and occasional war games on Hadley Common at Barnet. The consequence of this was that I was unable to visit Father as frequently as before. Life was becoming rather hectic so I left the Scouts.

The summer of 1944 was very pleasant. The V1 doodlebugs used to come over occasionally, but German air activity had virtually ceased as we had air supremacy. The weather was settled and warm and any spare time I had was spent either swimming or playing tennis with members of the gang at the recreational area on the Glebelands Swan Lane complex. Numbers were gradually depleted as individuals were called up. Every time somebody was due to go we had a special celebration at Totteridge. By this time we had made our peace with the local bobby, who was really a nice old boy shortly due for retirement. He was old enough to be our father and kept a paternal eye on us, even accepting the odd pint, quietly disappearing behind the pub to drink it. Surprisingly, we were never challenged about under-age drinking, although he must have had a very good idea about our ages. Policing was a bit more lenient in those days.

Even the girls were going into the services, and both Margery and Elizabeth joined the WAAF at about the same time. As I was one of the youngest members of our group, I could not wait for my call-up date, afraid that the war would be over before I got in. When I did go in October 1944, there were only about three people left. One of them was a haemophiliac. He was rejected as medically unfit. An unwelcome change to my call-up date, originally scheduled for 1 July 1944, occurred in the early summer. I received a letter to say that because pilot training courses were being discontinued no new entries were being accepted. However, as I had already been accepted as a CW candidate I was offered a transfer to the Royal Navy on the same terms. I accepted and waited for a revised call-up date, which was eventually identified as 16 October.

As I had already given formal notice to the gas company on the basis of my first date and my replacement had already been recruited, I found myself in danger of being unemployed for possibly three months. I needed a temporary job so I signed on again at the Labour Exchange. They offered me a job as a labourer at Maw's Pharmaceutical Company, New Barnet. It was a shock when on the first day I discovered that they manufactured, amongst other things, condoms. After manufacture these were individually tested by women and girls who sat in front of air test points. Each condom was placed over an outlet, inflated, and held at a set pressure to check for leaks. My job was to supply boxes of untested goods to the test lines and move the tested ones away for final packing. There were very few men in the factory, and no male youngsters at all. Being as unsure as I was with women, and getting a lot of ribald stick from them, I had a miserable time. The only bright spot was that I was paid about three times the wage that I had received at the gas company. My call-up date of 16 October came as a relief. Our gang being now so depleted my call-up celebration was relatively quiet compared to those that took place when our group first got together. Sadly, we never all managed to get together again.

6

Able Seaman (Met):
1944-45

After initial induction tests the CW candidates underwent training at Skegness for six weeks. This was followed by four months' specialist training at HMS *Raleigh*, Torpoint, near Plymouth, Devon. Survivors from this would go to the officer cadet "finishing school" at HMS *King Alfred*, Hove, to polish up the arts of being an officer and gentleman. It was nicknamed the "Knife and Fork" course. Most young officers were being trained up to man landing craft for the anticipated forthcoming invasion of Japan and Japanese held possessions in the Far East.

The naval establishment at Skegness was the pre-war Butlins holiday camp, which made an ideal training establishment. Situated on the east coast, it was a particularly bleak place where it rained and the wind blew continuously for the whole time we were there. CW candidates were placed in the tender care of an old petty officer long since retired but recalled to become an instructor. His pet hate was officers so we were subjected to three weeks of degrading treatment by a man who proudly claimed that he was the only person in the Navy who could prove he was sane. At some time during his career he had been an inmate in a mental institution and on discharge was given a clearance certificate. This he always carried around with him and at the drop of a hat would produce it to prove his point. Under his "fatherly" tuition the English language took on a whole new meaning and we were introduced to unfamiliar meanings to words like tart, rubber and dose.

We were thankful to escape from Skegness but at least we had the rudiments of service discipline and drilling under our belts. We had lost several of our initial intake as a result of the many and various tests to which we had been subjected. The survivors, thirty-two in all, went to HMS *Raleigh* at Torpoint, where training proper commenced. We learned all about seamanship, navigation, gunnery, sailing, signalling, how to march long distances and perform on the assault course twice a week. Above all, we learned about camaraderie. It was all very exciting and interesting for a seventeen-year-old and I enjoyed every minute of it. We

David, 1944

were also introduced to the local "scrumpy" cider, which was potent, and found the white flash worn on the cap to signify we were cadets was a great bird puller.

An incident occurred at Christmas 1944 which cast a shadow on the proceedings. At the last moment it was decided to keep one watch on duty over the holiday. Our watch was unlucky enough to be picked but the authorities decided to allow us shore leave as a sweetener. Four of us, who had become buddies, went into Plymouth for the evening and consumed a lot of scrumpy, which was an acquired taste, catching the last ferry back across the Tamar. We had about two miles to walk back to camp. One of our party, who was the son of a vicar, was unable to walk so two of us had to virtually carry him back to camp. The fourth member of our party decided to visit the Wrenery, which we had to pass, to look for his girlfriend (who was actually on leave). He climbed up a fire escape and wandered through the building waking everyone up. The upshot was all the lights coming on and loud screams from the girls, which we could hear further down the road as we struggled with our inert companion. Soon we heard someone running and our absent member caught up, proud of the fact that he had picked up some 'souvenirs' during his detour.

We managed to get back into camp with our drunk, the duty officer turning a blind eye to our state. The following morning there, for all to see, was a Wren service issue bra and underpants flying from the yardarm! The souvenirs had reached their final destination. It was only a matter of time before the four of us were hauled up and questioned. None of us would split on who was responsible, claiming total ignorance. The culprit finally confessed and was dismissed off the course. The rest of us were disciplined, told our conduct was unbecoming of potential officers and our card was marked. A nice Christmas Eve present!

We finished the course and were not surprised at the end of it to be told we had failed. The sweetener was that, except for two, everyone else failed as well. The explanation was simple. The European war was over. There were sufficient personnel released to man landing craft to go to the Far East so we were all surplus to requirements. The CW entry scheme came to a halt from then on. I considered I was very fortunate to have got that far.

I left Cornwall much fitter, half a stone heavier from good food and more worldly than I had been a few months earlier.

We returned to Skegness to remuster. Nothing much had changed except that our petty officer was missing from the scene. A crowd of New Zealanders, who had come to the UK to join the Navy – reason unknown – were not so tolerant as his earlier victims. They threw him into the empty swimming pool and put him in hospital. Skegness was a brighter place without him.

Whilst waiting for a posting, the New Zealanders challenged us to a "friendly" game of rugby. A scratch British team was raised, myself included. Even though most of us had played before, it was an absolute massacre. Before the game was over several of our side were off the pitch with various injuries, one or two actually ending up in sick bay. We agreed afterwards that it was just as well it was only a "friendly". It transpired that the New Zealanders had all served in the Army and seen active service in the Far East. They had decided to volunteer for the Royal Navy when the opportunity arose, seeing it as an easier option. They were, when we got to know them, a very nice crowd but tough as old boots with a total disregard for what they saw as petty discipline. I often wondered where they ended up as they had been selected for CW training, which was closed down shortly after I left Skegness.

I was fortunate enough to be selected for an intensive

course in meteorology so within a few days was transferred to the Fleet Air Arm base HMS *Daedalus* at Havant. Whilst there I applied to join a Combined Operations unit called Mobile Operational Naval Air Base – MONAB for short. The purpose of these units was to establish landing strips behind the main invasion forces so that carrier-based planes could operate from forward ground positions. In due course I went to Middle Wallop where a MONAB was forming up, arriving on VE Day, 9 May 1945.

A MONAB comprised about 400 personnel of all trades. Because of the high level of casualties expected whilst operating in the Far East, everyone had to have more than one trade. I opted to become a transport driver and had great fun driving 3-ton trucks around the airfield. In addition, we all had to have a proficiency in handling weapons. A small group of cut-throat RN Commandos was attached to our unit and took us through our paces with the .303 rifle and Sten guns. The Sten, although a very close quarter rapid-fire weapon, was cheap and cheerful and needed careful handling. On one occasion I dropped my gun in the firing pits and even though the safety catch was on it emptied the entire contents of the magazine. The instructor and I broke all speed records getting under cover and I was lucky not to be put on a charge.

The rumours were that we were heading to the Pacific to take part in the invasion of Japan with the Americans. We finally sailed on the SS *Otranto*, a converted peacetime cruise liner, then operating as a troopship. We sailed through the Mediterranean, the Suez Canal, the Red Sea, through to Colombo in what was then Ceylon, and finally across the Indian Ocean to Perth, Australia.

The trip itself was fairly uneventful. We stopped off at Colombo long enough to take a bus ride up to Candy, which was a hair-raising experience. The bus, crowded with peasants and livestock, lurched around hairpin bends with no regard for passenger comfort. Instead of slowing down through villages, the driver sat on his horn and accelerated. Pedestrians, chickens and pigs went flying in all directions. The trip back was as exciting.

We also had a large number of New Zealand and Australian ex-prisoners of war who were being repatriated. They had been given all their back pay in England before embarkation and spent the entire voyage gambling. Very large sums of money were involved but, although gambling was illegal on board ship, the Captain turned a blind eye to what was going on. He could hardly miss it as little groups of men could be found huddled together in all odd corners, oblivious to everything going on around them. The result was that a few arrived home very well off indeed but the majority were cleaned out. They were a pretty hard bunch and we tended to steer clear of them. As it was, there were quite a few fights during the voyage as old scores were settled.

We had the usual Crossing the Line ceremony, which provided a bit of light relief and just before reaching Western Australia we sailed through a hurricane. The *Otranto* was about 22,000 tons but she was tossed around like a cork and her decks were swept by thousands of gallons of sea water. Anything not securely lashed down went overboard. There were a lot of spare meals to be had during this period and, because I was not affected by sea-sickness, I did very well indeed.

We docked at Perth about 10 July and were, as it turned out, ill advisedly all allowed shore leave. Apart from the Australians and New Zealanders, who went completely out of control, the rest of the shipboard troops could not handle the strong drink available. In consequence, the Military Police had a wonderful time touring Perth and Freemantle with lorries just loading the inert bodies aboard and depositing them back at the ship's gangplanks. The following day the local population opened their houses to anyone who wanted hospitality. Jack Reid and I met up with a couple of lovely English expatriates of about sixty who fed us with masses of food and wanted to know everything about England. They treated us like royalty and could not do enough for us. One of them subsequently wrote to my mother to say how much they had enjoyed meeting us.

We sailed again next day for Sydney, arriving about four days later. We immediately disembarked and were transported to HMS *Golden Hind* which was a tented transit camp on one of Sydney's racecourses to the west of the city. We were told that all our transport and equipment was being transferred to a fleet escort carrier HMS *Slinger* and we would be moving on within a few days - destination unknown, but rumour said it was to be the Philippines. In the meantime we were allowed shore leave every day and we all made the most of it.

Sydney was a bustling city with a lot of American influence in those days. There seemed to be no shortage of petrol judging by the number of cars on the roads, many of them American. Food rationing was unheard of and lots of exotic fruit was available. We had a wonderful time exploring the eating places and bars in town, all of which were closed at 6 p.m. sharp. We went out to Manly and Bondi beaches to enjoy the sun and the views. The American bikini was much in evidence and we were still wearing heavy khaki battledress! One thing we had not been issued with was tropical kit. It was probably because the powers that be did not want us to know which way we were going. We were better dressed to go south to the Antarctic than north.

The hub of service life in Sydney was the British Centre, a club open to all ranks where food and "soft drinks" were available. It was remarkable how strong these drinks were and it was normal to stagger off back to camp at peace with the world. On one occasion we got back to our tent to find a large green object about two feet high standing in the middle of the tent. We all thought it was about time to be signing the pledge when we discovered that it was a Praying Mantis, an oversized grasshopper indigenous to Australia.

A couple of us took up an offer, via the British Centre, to visit a farm in the Blue Mountains. We were picked up by a very pleasant couple one morning and driven for a couple of hours through lovely scenery to their cattle farm. By Australian standards it was quite small but their lifestyle was very comfortable and they were again very keen to find out all about England and what conditions had been like during the war. The husband was a first generation Australian, his parents having moved out from England at the turn of the century when he was quite young.

The only downside to our stay was the attitude of Australian servicemen to British and, in particular, American personnel. Hyde Park in the centre of the city was to be avoided after dark, especially if in the company of a girl. There were a number of reported cases of people being beaten up. The problem was understandable in the context that many Australians had a bad war in New Guinea and did not take kindly to strangers monopolizing their women.

Our stay in Sydney passed all too quickly and by about 24 July we were on our way again. We made a quick stop at Brisbane and I was fortunate enough to be part of a work detail to go ashore to pick up some small items of equipment. From what I saw of the city, it was very different from Sydney. We pushed on at best speed, passing to the east of New Guinea to our next port of call – Manus Island – to refuel. This is a flat, volcanic island with very little vegetation. During the war it was used as a fuel and water depot for Allied shipping. The tenders came alongside our ship, crewed by dark skinned "natives". When they spoke to us we discovered that they were members of an earlier MONAB who had been stationed there for some months. They were desperate to get off the island and we felt very sorry for them. We had visions of ending up in a similar position on some remote Pacific island miles from anywhere.

Very soon after leaving Manus we started to be shadowed by a Japanese seaplane. It was an enormous aircraft powered by six engines. It obviously knew that we were not carrying aircraft and always flew out of range of our anti-aircraft armament, which comprised several banks of twin Oerlikons. To maintain morale, we were allowed to fire off at will once a day. Anyone who wanted to could volunteer to man the guns so we all had a go. We never did find out where the Jap seaplane was based and after a few days it disappeared.

As we neared the Philippines, we started picking up quite a lot of shipping moving in and out of Manila. In the early hours of 6 August 1945 we dropped anchor in Manila Bay to join an enormous fleet of warships, transports and merchant vessels being assembled for the invasion of Japan. We were looking forward to getting a few hours ashore in Manila. Our journey up from Australia had been hot and uncomfortable. Apart from the normal ship's crew, there was our entire MONAB of 400-plus and all our equipment. Bulldozers, trucks, lorries, jeeps and heavy breakdown vehicles packed the areas below decks normally housing aircraft. The ship's company slept in hammocks in any odd corner which could be found.

Within a few hours of our arrival, the news was flashed to all ships in the harbour that a new, very powerful bomb had been dropped on Hiroshima. Every ship erupted with cheering. No one was in any doubt about the morality of it at that moment; they could only see the end of the war in sight and the saving of countless thousands of lives.

7

Hong Kong: 1945-46

That same day we received orders to put to sea again and finally joined a small force of destroyers, minesweepers and a cruiser heading towards Hong Kong about 800 miles away. We arrived off the Colony by 12 August and although the Japanese had stopped fighting and were negotiating with the Allies, they had not surrendered.

In the early hours of 13 August we sailed into Hong Kong harbour, through a channel swept by the minesweepers, and anchored on the Kowloon side. At first light shore patrols were detailed to land and search Kowloon for any prisoners of war or civilian internees who, it was believed, were in the area. Similar patrols were going ashore from other ships onto Victoria Island. We had instructions not to fire on any Japanese troops sighted unless we were under threat. Our patrol, led by a young officer, had to work its way from the railway station up the Nathan Road. The shops were built out over the pavements so we were able to find plenty of cover. Everything was deserted, no one about, all the shops closed and shuttered. We didn't see a soul, it was eerie. Had the population gone underground? Had they left the city? There were two things that impressed themselves on us: one was the constant tolling of a church bell a long way off, the other was a sickly sweet smell, which pervaded the atmosphere. We couldn't place it.

Suddenly we spotted a Japanese army patrol marching down the road straight towards us. They made no attempt to take cover and we all thought, "This is it." The lieutenant gave the command "Safety catches off; fire when I give the order." By this time we had stopped and taken up defensive positions behind whatever cover we could find and waited. To our utter astonishment the Japs, who had obviously seen us, marched straight past us without as much as a look. It was obvious the ceasefire was holding. We carried on with our patrol up Nathan Road until we received orders via a mobile W/T set we were carrying to return to Kowloon ferry. We did not know at the time that we were very close to the Royal Observatory, which was the Japanese Headquarters. Further up the road, past the Observatory, was an internment camp at Sham Shui Po.

When we got back to the ship, we met with other patrols. Some had been dropped in the Kowloon dock area, which was a shambles. A few weeks earlier the Americans had bombed the area intensively and there had been a lot of casualties, both Japanese and civilian. Little attempt had

The Governor's House as seen from nearby service billet, 1947

been made to clear the dead from the ruins, hence the smell we had been unable to place. Also the place was alive with vermin. Someone was going to have a nice job sorting that lot out. The boys who had been into this area were visibly affected by what they had seen.

The following day, 14 August, the Japanese formally surrendered. Our MONAB was immediately moved up to Kai Tak aerodrome. The Americans had also given this a pasting and the runway was pitted with deep craters, numerous aircraft had been destroyed and most of the buildings had been razed to the ground. It was totally un-operational. Ours was the ideal unit to get it back into service. Our transport – including the bulldozers – was soon at work. The wrecked aircraft were pulled clear and piled in heaps. The bulldozers were employed in filling in the bomb craters and, as soon as a stable surface had been achieved, we laid the rolls of metal matting over the whole area. The intention was to get the first aircraft in as soon as possible.

We had been hard at work for about three days when all the Meteorological staff were pulled out and sent to the Royal Observatory. Our brief was to get it operational as soon as possible. The Japanese had been rounded up and taken off to a POW camp. We checked out the buildings and found the place in chaos. The place appeared to have been "turned over" by the British troops who had initially occupied the Observatory so there was really nothing of value left. We did, however, make a very unpleasant discovery. In the grounds was a deep air-raid shelter, which had been used as a toilet by the Japanese. The smell was overpowering. Less unpleasant finds included a box and a book. The box was full of Japanese occupation money – totally worthless but we all took some as souvenirs. The book was a dog-eared copy by the late Victorian editor Frank Harris, author of the famous *My Life and Loves*. It subsequently joined our technical reference library and was borrowed by anyone who wanted to fine-tune their sexual skills. How it came to be in the Observatory was always a mystery. We had to assume that the first troops to enter the Japanese Headquarters were not into Victorian literature and had discarded it as of no interest. Their loss!

We soon found out why the Japs had used the shelter as a toilet. The sewerage disposal systems were not working, presumably as a result of the American bombing. Fortunately we still had water and electricity.

As we arrived at the Royal Observatory with only our kit and some army field rations, we had to do something fairly quickly. So we took off into local houses and "scrounged" everything we needed, beds, cooking utensils, any tinned food, etc. As the area was deserted we had no compunction about doing it.

At the same time we were joined by some RAF personnel, radio operators and a Flight Lieutenant Met Officer who took "nominal" charge. We gradually became aware of our immediate colleagues. Three stood out for sheer character and high spirits, Ted Woodruffe, Stan Green and Pete Symons. I cannot remember them on the journey out from England but they must have been on MONAB 8. They were all ex-aircrew under training (as was Jack Reid) whose courses had been closed down and they had remustered into Meteorology. Very soon teleprinter links with the Royal Naval base at Stonecutter Island, and the airport, were established. We had brought all our own met gear on the MONAB and this was transferred from HMS *Slinger* and we were in business! We worked shifts over a 24-hour period and issued forecasts every three hours. At first the number of ground reporting stations was minimal and we had to rely on observations from service vessels dotted around the coastline of Asia. Gradually however we started picking up observations from ground stations all over the place. It was quite exciting to see how these increased during the next few weeks as one place after another started getting back to normal.

Whilst all this was going on we had some moments of light relief. To clear out the air-raid shelter, our CO requested and obtained the services of a Japanese working party. POWs were housed in camps outside Kowloon and were marched in daily to work on various projects, the biggest being the clearance of the dock area shambles. They used to be guarded by members of the 41st and 42nd Marine Commando Units, both of which had had a bloody time working their way down the Malay Peninsula. They enjoyed their job and would beat the living daylights out of any Japs who stepped out of line or could not keep up. Behind each column would follow a 3-ton truck and any injured Jap was thrown into the back. What happened to them we never bothered to inquire. There were already too many stories circulating about the atrocities they had committed during the occupation. Some of this we would later see for ourselves.

Our working party duly arrived at the RO headed by a Japanese officer, resplendent in polished leather boots, who spoke quite good English. He passed our instructions on to the non-com accompanying them with slaps to the face. The non-com in turn passed the instructions to the troops, also slapping them. At first we were amused to see this but decided enough was enough and told the officer to stop doing it. We split the working party up: one lot to dig a large pit in the grounds, the second to clear all the excrement out of the shelter to put in the pit. All went well until the officer started shouting and slapping his men again. We had had enough so lined the POWs up in front of the RO and told the officer to take his boots off in front of the men, then work barefooted with them in the shelter. He reacted violently to this and said he could not do it because of loss of face; please could he commit hara-kiri – the Japanese ritual suicide. We refused and the man became a gibbering wreck. At the end of the day when the POWs were collected, we told the escort troops what had happened and that we did not want him back. He never reappeared and the subsequent work parties operated quite happily without an officer. I think they knew that, compared with some of the work details, they had a relatively easy job. We were not sorry when they finally left, they were an evil crowd.

We had learned that the Japanese had carried out a repressive regime during the occupation. Many civilians had been murdered and a great number had fled the Colony into Southern China. The rest of the population were slowly starved. When news of the impending relief of the Colony reached the civilian population they went to ground to sit it out until the Allied troops arrived. The civilian internees who were released were living skeletons and the conditions they lived in were worse than one could imagine. As one of the camps was just up the road from the RO, we were able to see for ourselves just how terrible life had been for them. Digressing somewhat, when my daughter and I returned to Hong Kong in 1982 we visited this site, which was now a pleasant little park. No sign of the history of the place remained, not even a plaque.

Within weeks of the reoccupation, weekly trainloads of people and luggage started to arrive at Kowloon Railway Station. They came in from Southern China with passengers sitting on the carriage roofs and buffers and standing on the external running boards. How they cleared Customs in the New Territory remained a mystery. Whether they were all previous Hong Kong residents, we had no idea. As soon as the trains drew into the station, the hordes took off in all directions. Very soon shops started opening up, buildings were occupied and the Colony came to life. Shopkeepers were desperate to lay their hands on goods to sell. Our CO, with ever an eye open for a profitable line, suggested that we should help fuel the economy by redirecting NAAFI issues of food, drink and cigarettes and surplus service issue clothing. He argued that we would be doing everyone a favour including ourselves. Very soon we had established contact with some local shopkeepers and a regular supply line was set up. Three of our group became the contact men who negotiated prices based on the unit of a tin of 50 cigarettes, for which we obtained $1.50. Pete, who had a good head for figures as an ex-bank clerk, was one of the contacts. Soon, every week after dark, a convoy of rickshaws left the RO loaded with all the goodies. In return the boys returned with pockets full of dollars. Pete was official treasurer and set up a structured use for the money which was to include a cook, a couple of amahs to cover the general housework and washing, and a monthly party. Any surplus would be split equally amongst us all, officers included. We intended to live as comfortably as possible.

It was taken for granted that everyone would "play the game" but unfortunately a major snag arose when one of our contacts was caught cheating. We used to be able to buy blue naval serge through the Naval Stores. There were two qualities, English and Australian, which was much superior. Our enterprising contact took a roll of English cloth and wrapped some Australian material round it. He then took it downtown and sold it at the higher price. Naturally the merchant who was conned was very upset. He and some of our other customers arrived at the RO insisting on seeing "No. 1 Boss", the Flight Lieutenant. What happened was pure farce. The Chinese insisted that they would no longer do business with us if the contact was not fired. An agreement was reached and our man was "sent to Coventry" for being a cheat. Business resumed as honour on both sides was satisfied. It was just as well that everyone was involved in the black market activities otherwise a few heads would

Hong Kong showing the Japanese monument

have rolled if 'No. 1 Boss' had not been implicated.

About the same time as these activities were going on, preparations were being made to destroy a large memorial which the Japanese had erected on the top of one of the peaks on Victoria Island. It was to commemorate their capture of Hong Kong in 1942. It had been built by English and Australian POWs and survivors of the HK Defence Force, who had fought with great heroism before being overwhelmed. The Royal Engineers packed the base with high explosive and a date was set. All available Japanese POWs were lined up to watch along with thousands of allied servicemen and civilians. There was an enormous explosion and the memorial disappeared in a great cloud of dust and debris. Everyone, except the Japs, cheered like mad; nobody bothered to ask them how they felt about it, they were not worthy of consideration in view of what they had done during the occupation. Everyone hated them, and feeling was running high.

As soon as the RO was up and running we were given clearance to move further afield when we were off duty. We found a quiet little bay in the New Territory, at Castle Peak, with a cliff backdrop, and regularly borrowed a 30-cwt truck to go swimming and sunbathing. On the way there we used to pass through several villages where the livestock roamed free. We hatched a villainous plot to 'win' a piglet to relieve the monotony of our field rations. So, on the return trip one day, we saw a suitable victim on the outskirts of the village. Stopping the truck, four of us, including myself, jumped out and tried to catch it. Unfortunately it took off, squealing its head off. The noise alerted the whole village and an angry crowd came racing down the road after us waving some pretty fearsome weapons. In desperation we brought our rugby skills to play and captured it. Getting it into the back of the truck was another problem but we finally made it just before we were overwhelmed by the crowd. By now our consciences were giving us trouble so we threw some dollars onto the road and roared off. That evening we had a wonderful feast of roast pork prepared for us by, of all people, the Sikh wireless operators. As none of us had tasted fresh meat for weeks, they did not allow their religious taboos to worry them.

Another incident occurred on a later trip to this beach. On arrival, we parked alongside a Royal Naval jeep, had our swim and packed up to come back to the RO. On trying to start the truck we found we were almost out of fuel. Our CO, who was with us, authorised the removal of a jerry can of petrol from the jeep, the contents of which were poured into our truck. It wouldn't start due to an airlock in the fuel line so we removed the air filter and I started priming the carburettor with petrol.

Unfortunately the driver tried to start the engine whilst I was still doing this, the engine backfired and the carburettor burst into flames. I threw the burning jerry can away from me as I jumped clear, and we used our fire extinguisher to put out the flames. Someone suddenly noticed that the jeep alongside us was on fire as well. By a stroke of bad luck, the jerry can had landed underneath the rear of the jeep and set it alight. We frantically pushed our truck out of the way but by this time the jeep was blazing out of control, and eventually blew up. Whilst we were standing around looking at the mess, the jeep's owner appeared, a very irate Naval Commander, and obviously his Chinese girlfriend. They had been otherwise occupied further down the beach and had been unaware of what was going on. All of us managed to get a lift back to Kowloon in an Army lorry, which towed our truck. We sat in the back of the lorry for twenty miles in stony silence. The Commander threatened to have our CO court-martialled but nothing was ever heard of the incident. We decided that he was taking unauthorised shore leave with his girlfriend and couldn't make an issue of it.

Because of our contacts with the Chinese community, when the time came to employ a Chinese cook and amahs we were introduced to some very satisfactory staff. We were by this time obtaining food supplies from the Naval Dockyard on Victoria Island. The CO also negotiated an allowance to employ a cook rather than use our fund. In consequence, we obtained the services of an excellent cook, quite young but able to do marvels with our rations supplemented with local purchases. We never found out about his background but he had been "vetted" before coming to us. The two amahs were sisters, young girls in their late teens. Their parents had been killed by the Japs and they had fled to relatives in China. They were much better class and had been convent educated but were traumatised by what had happened to their family. A house rule was agreed by general consent: the girls were "off limits". They stayed with us for the whole period we were in Hong Kong and no one ever broke the rule. For some time after they joined us, because of the likelihood of them being propositioned, or worse, we escorted them daily to and from their accommodation in Kowloon. They saw us as extended

A view of the Governor's House through the gateway

family and nothing was too much trouble for them. We never had to darn another pair of socks! When we left Hong Kong, we made sure they were fixed up with new jobs.

While at Kai Tak I had met an RAF photographer called George and the meeting had a certain advantage. There were a number of Waafs also stationed at the aerodrome and we needed to contact them to come to our first party, which was imminent. George was on the spot so I invited him and some of his pals on the understanding that they would bring at least a similar number of girls. The great day dawned, food and drink was ready and the guests arrived – about thirty of them! They were like locusts, didn't bring a thing and ate and drank everything in sight. They even took over our sleeping accommodation and we had to turf a lot off our own beds when it was time to close down. A post mortem the following day voted the evening a disaster mainly because our boys had not been able to split the party up and get to know the girls better. We needed to rethink our strategy for the future.

The parties continued on a monthly basis but we were

much more selective about who we invited. George and his male pals were quietly dropped. We still invited a small number of Waafs but also got a few Wrens along. They were now stationed at the Naval Dockyard mainly on administration and communications. We had been alerted to their presence when someone had tried the usual service "banter" with the teleprinter operator at Stonecutter Island only to be told in no uncertain terms that there were now Wrens operating them – so please could we clean up our act! Great excitement amongst our gang as we could now tap another source, which was followed up with alacrity. No long-term relationships developed. The girls were really only interested in trying to collect an officer as a future husband, but they were good fun. As I was not a heavy drinker, I was nominated to be one of the regular barmen. I have a picture taken of the bar where I look about "seven sheets to the wind". I must have been sampling the quality before the party.

A spin-off from the first party was the growing friendship between George and Jack Reid. Jack was very interested in photography and also a film buff. Later, when the Hong Kong papers got back into business, both of them became film critics. This took up a lot of their off-duty time and I saw much less of Jack. I, in my turn, had gravitated into the group comprising Stan Green, Ted Woodruffe and Pete Symons. They were determined to live life in the fast lane. This included sampling the many bars that were opening up and getting better acquainted with some of the local girls. In this last respect, I found myself at a disadvantage. I was the youngest member of the RO and riddled with religious barriers against sex before marriage. Also I had a healthy respect for the very real dangers of VD, which became rampant in the Colony. The Japanese, notorious for their sexual activities, had infected a high proportion of the female population that remained in the Colony during the occupation, but had not provided treatment for civilians. The health of girls coming back into Hong Kong from China was also suspect, so anyone using their services ran a very high risk of infection. The authorities tried to counter by putting lurid posters up all over the Colony with pictures showing the effect of the disease. I decided early on that the risk was just not worth it; a view, I have to say, not shared by the greatest majority of the service population. A walk down Wan Chai, the Red Light district on Victoria Island, was an eye-opener on degraded human behaviour. Sadly, several of our crowd got infected and were taken off to hospital never to be seen again. It was not only the "other ranks" who took part in these activities. My CO, with whom I worked on shift, he as the forecaster, and me as an observer and plotter, set himself up in a flat with a Chinese mistress. He never slept in the RO and when we were on nights he would creep into the office to do the first early morning forecast looking terrible. He found his active lifestyle debilitating and reckoned he would have to go into training to keep up with his young girlfriend.

A consequence of his absence from the Met Office meant that I used to do quite a bit more than the other observers. I used to outline the pressure gradients and frontal systems which the CO would work on in more detail and produce a forecast. One morning he was later on duty than normal. As bad luck would have it, a request came through on the teleprinter from Kai Tak for a flight forecast to Kuala Lumpur. For all the information available for Burma and Malaya, they might have been on a different planet. I was in a dilemma. I could not officially inform Kai Tak that our CO was missing from duty so I did the next best thing. I cobbled up a forecast to the best of my ability and passed it on with fingers crossed. I suggested on the forecast that a check should be made with Singapore, who might have more information than us. When I next saw my CO I told him what I had done. He was amused by what had happened.

The sequel to this came about a month later. The CO and I were on duty during the day when a jeep drove up and out got a Fleet Air Arm Lieutenant Commander pilot. He was obviously very upset and demanded to know who was on duty on the day in question. The CO had to admit that he was. The story that unfolded was that weather conditions had been nothing like the forecast. The flight of six planes had run into heavy thunderstorms and had been forced to divert and make emergency landings to refuel. In vain did the CO show him the map and explain that it was out of our area and meteorological reports were minimal. Our pilot was not impressed. To give him his due, the CO took all the blame but luckily no official action was taken against him. The two of us had a long talk after the pilot left. It was agreed that such a situation should never happen again and he would always ensure that he was on duty on time in the future. It was a promise he kept for the rest of our stay in Hong Kong. After that he and I became good friends and worked very well together. I learned a lot of theory about forecasting from him, information that was very useful when I subsequently went to Antarctica a couple of years later.

After a while we started hearing stories of an ancient Chinese walled village in the New Territory so a party of us decided to go and have a look at it. Having only vague directions and no map, it took us quite a while to find it. We actually smelt it before we saw it. The public refuse tip was outside the walls and was alive with fleas and rodents. We had a quick look inside the village but the absolute abject poverty, and smell, drove us back. The peasants who lived in the village were in a worse state than we had seen anywhere else. We felt that our presence was intrusive, as we had only come to look not to help, so we quickly left.

We understood that during the Japanese occupation any female babies were killed at birth because the parents only wanted male children. We could picture them being thrown onto the refuse tip and subsequently eaten by the pigs. We found out later that it was a normal practice in China to kill off unwanted female babies on economic grounds.

From the village we drove up to the border crossing into China. It was guarded by soldiers who were scrutinising everyone coming into the Colony. Anyone who had not got the correct documentation was turned back. It appeared that already the Authorities were concerned about the great numbers of people who had flooded back from China. The economy of the Colony could not support uncontrolled entry.

Towards the end of the year we heard that Chiang Kai-shek was losing his battle with the Communists and was retreating towards Hong Kong. He negotiated with the British and Americans and it was agreed that he could cross the border and march to the Kowloon docks. Here his forces and equipment would be shipped by the Americans to Manchuria.

The appointed day arrived in October and a large crowd of interested spectators watched a motley army shamble through Kowloon to the docks. A lot had no footwear at all and most were in ragged uniforms. Their equipment looked pretty archaic and everything, including livestock, was carried in wicker baskets on long poles. Suddenly, in the middle of the column, which had been passing for a couple of hours, we spotted some lorries in fairly good condition. They looked vaguely familiar. They should have done as they still had MONAB 8 markings on them! It subsequently transpired that when the MONAB had finished at Kai Tak it was disbanded, most of the personnel going to Stonecutter Island to be remustered. Most of the transport was surplus to requirements so the Transport Officer had done a deal with the

Chinese and sold it to them at a handsome profit. The trouble was that the deal was illegal and most of the profit went into the officer's own pocket. He never anticipated that the vehicles would turn up again. When he heard the army was coming to Hong Kong he must have known the game was up. Needless to say, he was court-martialled, dismissed from the Service and jailed. He also lost all his profit, a very nice flat and a mistress.

After about three months the Colony was well on the way to normality. At the Observatory we were, to all intents and purposes, seconded to the civilian Meteorological Service. The Navy provided us with pay, NAAFI facilities and "slops" (clothing) but had no other interest in us. So we became civilians and never wore uniforms, except to collect our dues at the Naval Dockyard. We had money in our pockets, which was supplemented by our black market activities, and had a very comfortable lifestyle. The same applied to the RAF personnel and we all got on very well together. Cricket and hockey teams were raised and played regularly. I was not interested in cricket but enjoyed hockey. Several of the games we played were against Indian servicemen who were much more skilled than us but unfailingly polite, always cheering us if we scored. This comfortable lifestyle continued until we handed over officially to civilian staff and left Hong Kong on 11 July 1946.

8

Snapshots and Memories: 1946-47

A series of snapshots remain in my mind from life in Hong Kong and later:

1. Lord Mountbatten, who was Commander-in-Charge Far East, finally issued an order of the day instructing everyone to treat the Japanese POWs humanely as required by the Geneva Convention. It was too late to save hundreds who died.

2. I obtained a genuine Rolex watch for a knock-down price very early on. It would have been worth a small fortune back home. On board ship coming back to the UK, I played deck hockey. Because of widespread pilfering on the ship, I wore the watch during the game. The padre of the 42nd Marine Commandos, who was on the opposite side, took an almighty swipe at the puck, missed and hit my wrist. The watch ended up in a hundred pieces. Was it divine intervention? Or retribution?

3. I was walking down the Nathan Road in a crowded street when two men pushed past me and came alongside another man just in front of me. Both produced

revolvers, shot him and disappeared into the crowd. One look at the body satisfied me he was dead; half his face was blown off. I did not stop, neither did anyone else. Many old scores from the occupation were settled the same way. Or it could have been the criminal fraternity, the Tong, having a sort out.

4. One of our RAF drivers, who was a bit of a sadist, used to delight in telling us how he played tag with the Chinese coolies. They used to carry everything, including excrement for manure, in two wicker baskets suspended at opposite ends of a long bamboo pole. They would jog along the open road from Kowloon to Kai Tak to their smallholdings. He would drive slowly up behind one and deliberately knock the back basket, which would swing round, unbalance the coolie and shoot his load all over the road. The trick was to accelerate away fast enough to avoid spillage all over the truck. Most found his stories unacceptable and, in consequence, he was shunned.

5. Chinese funerals were conducted out of town. The coffin used to be suspended between two poles and a team of eight bearers would carry it to the burial ground near Kai Tak, followed by all the mourners on foot. It was quite a long way and it was normal for the entire party to stop at an appropriate place and have a "brew up". What better place to sit than on the coffin?

6. A lot of places were "off limits" to servicemen, either because they were brothels or sold contaminated food. The 41st and 42nd Marine Commandos had the job of policing Kowloon and were, in the main, a load of thugs. They had already gained a reputation for beating up Japanese POWs. We always suspected that there was a racket, as places seemed to be closing down one day and

Cigarette factory Chinese style – he rolls 'em from butts collected in the streets!

open again shortly after. Strangely enough this view was confirmed some years later when I found myself working with the man who had been the Provost Marshal of Kowloon at the time we were there. He used to boast about the amount of money he had made. If a brothel or restaurant did not pay protection money they were closed down. As soon as they paid up, they were allowed to re-open.

7. It was surprising how many shopkeepers spoke English at varying levels of efficiency. We never had any problems over communication. Also, they all used the abacus, the predecessor to the calculator. It comprised several horizontal rows of beads, which could be moved along a rod. It used a unit of ten and could multiply, divide, add and subtract at very high speed in the hands of a skilled operator.

8. Whilst Chiang Kai-shek was still fighting in South China, transport planes piloted by Chinese Nationalists

would fly into Hong Kong to refuel and pick up cargo before flying on to China. The pilots never seemed to worry about freight weights and, in consequence, there were regular crashes at Kai Tak. The backdrop to the aerodrome was a range of mountains and the planes just could not make the necessary altitude and flew straight into them. Later the RAF based a permanent Mountain Rescue Team at Kai Tak.

9. At regular intervals meteorological flights used to fly out of Kai Tak checking, particularly, upper air conditions of temperature, wind speed, humidity and cloud formation. Aircraft fitted with special instruments included a Dakota and Barracuda torpedo bomber. Occasionally we had the opportunity to volunteer to act as the Meteorological observer. The Barracuda was a two-seater, the observer sitting behind the pilot in what was essentially a perspex blister. The floor was perspex to accommodate a bomb/torpedo aiming position. The canopy was an astrodome to allow unobstructed view for

Newspaper seller, 1947

carrying out astral fixes. I flew in this aircraft several times and never felt very comfortable.

There was one pilot in particular who would delight in coming on to his landing approach very fast – and then dropping the plane down onto the runway. I'm sure he did it to scare the life out of his passenger – in my case he was successful.

10. Kowloon – Victoria Island ferries were a well-known feature and picked their way across a very busy strip of water avoiding dozens of junks, small boats and warships. They were the only link to the mainland and carried everything from people to pigs. They were always overcrowded but there were no accidents during the time we were there.

11. Once on shore on Victoria Island, there were two main forms of transport: the rickshaw, of which there were hundreds, and trains, which provided a cheap and efficient service around the Island. There were few buses initially because there was no petrol available for civilian use, but they started to appear on the roads before we left. Many of the poorer people had no option but to walk everywhere.

12. The Chinese population were genuinely pleased to see British servicemen in the Colony. They represented liberation from a cruel oppressor, and a constant source of supply of essential commodities such as cigarettes. This attitude was in stark contrast to the pre-war white British population who survived the occupation. After a spell out of the Colony for medical treatment and leave, they started to return to their former jobs. They brought with them the arrogance and bigotry of the old British Empire colonials. They treated "other ranks" service

personnel with disdain. They were not liked in the heady post-war days when Labour had ousted a long run of pre-war Conservative governments.

13. A Forces Educational Centre and Social Club was opened up for service personnel of all ranks. It included a library run by two members of the Field Army Nursing Yeomanry (FANYs), one of whom was very attractive. Needless to say the library was an immediate success and there were always lots of servicemen hanging around to admire the view. Rumours had it that she only dated officers and was "off limits" to other ranks. One of our officer forecasters dated her a few times but she had expensive tastes and he could not stand the pace. She left Hong Kong before us and we thought she had passed into history. At the end of 1946, however, when Pete, Stan, Ted and I were doing our educational training course, we came across a newspaper story about her. She had decided to come back to the UK via America and had taken ship passage to the western seaboard. Working her way across country, she had taken part in a TV show, which she had won and picked up a lot of money. There was a picture of her coming down the gangplank at Southampton to be greeted by her fiancé, who looked a most insignificant fellow. We fell about laughing and wondered if she told him what she really got up to in Hong Kong.

14. I was fortunate enough to get some very good photographs during my stay. What stands out is the tremendous difference in standards between the coolie labourers and city workers who all appeared to have stepped out of a Saville Row tailor. Tailoring was cheap but initially cloth was difficult to come by.

15. In the spring of 1946, pre-war employees at the Royal Observatory started drifting back. It was now only a matter of time before they took over from us and we would be on our way home. They started working alongside us, catching up on the new procedures. They were a mixture of Chinese and Portuguese. The Head of the Meteorological Service was British, as were some of his senior staff, and they were all in position by the end of June.

On 10 July 1946 we quit the RO and boarded HMS *Queen*, another American-built escort carrier. We were heading for Colombo. We sailed the day before a terrible hurricane hit the Colony. Winds were gusting to 70–80 miles an hour when we left. We later heard that, when the epicentre of the storm passed through, hundreds of junks, which had run for shelter in Aberdeen, were destroyed along with most of the shantytown that had sprung up in that area. The death toll was high, the authorities having no real idea of the numbers who perished. It was a sombre end to what had been a wonderful experience for us all. We all left with good memories and, in many ways, were sorry to go. We were going to return to a very drab, impoverished England with an uncertain future ahead of us. Of my immediate group of friends, Pete was returning to the bank he had worked in before joining up; Ted wanted to become a journalist, he had a way with words; Stan was a talented artist and wanted to do further training; Jack was not sure what to do but thought he would like to see a bit more of the world before settling down. He was good with a camera and had ideas of using his flair as a basis of a career. For myself, I was interested in forestry and had taken a correspondence course on the subject with Sydney University. I had also applied to several universities in Scotland and Wales, which ran degree courses. We all wondered how near we would get to our targets.

We duly arrived at Colombo where we were loaded with a full deck cargo of American Avenger Lend-Lease fighters. These could not go back to the States and were to be dumped overboard in the Indian Ocean. Before the aircraft went over the side, ship's company were allowed to take "souvenirs" off them. Everyone clambered over them and into the cockpits taking out anything which could be easily shifted. Eventually they were either pushed or craned over the side. It was not until about twenty-four hours later that it was discovered a sailor was missing. It was assumed that he was still in the cockpit of an aircraft when it was ditched. No attempt was made to carry out a search and rescue operation, the area was notorious for sharks and it was unlikely that he would have survived very long.

We eventually arrived back in England and were drafted to HMS *Daedalus*, where we stood out like sore thumbs in our khaki battledress. We got all sorts of comments such as "You do know the war is over don't you?" but we were rather proud of our uniform. In due course, Authority decreed that we had to be re-kitted to regulation blues.

It was obvious no one really knew what to do with us so Stan, Ted, Pete and I wangled a place on a de-mob educational training course. We had a wide range of subjects to choose from, and, interestingly, one of the RN instructors was one of the two cadets on our course who passed out from HMS *Raleigh* to HMS *King Alfred*. He was one of the scruffiest people I have ever met but he was a very good teacher.

Our course finished at the end of November 1946 and I was immediately posted to the Fleet Air Arm base at Yeovilton, which had been an aircrew-training establishment. The four of us made our farewells with a lot of sadness. We had shared some happy times together and we promised to keep in touch when we got into Civvy Street.

I spent four and a half months as a meteorologist at Yeovilton, until I was demobbed on 22 April 1947. This included final leave entitlement which I spent at home. That winter was one of the coldest on record. There was no flying during the whole of that period and the base was completely cut off by massive snowfalls and drifts for nearly two weeks. I actually quite enjoyed it there. I was my own boss. I had no hassle from anyone and it gave me the opportunity to gradually adjust from a structured service environment to the eventual return to civilian life without the camaraderie of my peers.

What happened to everyone back in Civvy Street?

Jack Reid did a spell in tea planting in Colombo after his trip to Antarctica. He later joined the Central Electricity Board as a Wayleave Officer. His job was to negotiate with landowners and local authorities for the routing of overhead and underground power lines. An unusual job. I met up with him late in 1987 at a get together of ex-FIDS and BAS personnel who had served at the Argentine Island base. He retired, aged 65, in 1991 and went to New Zealand with his wife for eighteen months to stay with one of their daughters.

Pete Symons went back to the bank. He later moved on to an international bank and served overseas in Africa and the Middle and Far East. I was best man at his wedding in 1947. Sadly he died of a heart attack aged 51. I never met him again after his wedding but we corresponded over the years.

Ted Woodruffe became a reporter with the Leominster News. He later became Sports Editor of the Hereford Times and was well known and respected in the sporting world. He died of a heart attack in Madeira in 1994, aged 67. He and his wife, Pat, Stan Green's sister, lived in Hereford all their married life. I last saw them in 1964, and only recently heard of his death from Stan. Reading through his obituaries, there was reference to the fact that he first developed an interest in journalism through working for the South China Post in Hong Kong in 1945. He probably submitted reports on the various sporting activities in which we were involved. It is strange that George, Jack and Ted should have been connected with the newspaper.

Stan Green went to art school when he was demobbed. For reasons I cannot remember he later became a policeman in Birmingham until his retirement. I met up with him and his wife, Ruth, several times in the 1960s. We lost contact until 1994 when I tracked him down to Redruth, Cornwall. We are hoping to have a belated reunion in the not too distant future.

Memories of Herefordshire 1947

Like many other ex-servicemen after the war I did not want to return to the city. A country life appealed, and I decided on Forestry.

Whilst still in Hong Kong I had applied for and been provisionally accepted for a Forestry degree course at Bangor University commencing autumn 1947. To prepare myself I had already taken a correspondence course on timber with Sydney University, but I still needed practical experience. In consequence I applied to the Forestry Commission and was accepted as a Forestry trainee. I was given a position on a large estate a few miles west of Hereford. I was to lodge with the estate shepherd, Bob Jones.

Early lambing coincided with late heavy snowfalls that year. In consequence most sheep were standing in deep snow and needed to be brought off the hills into shelter. On arrival at the shepherd's cottage I discovered that the large flagstone kitchen had been converted into a rescue area for the lambs. About twenty were laid out in front of the open range and Mrs Jones and her four children were busily engaged in bottle-feeding them.

For the first week I accompanied Bob every day with his two sheep dogs, and we recovered scores of lambs, some alive, many dead.

It was a brutal introduction into the ways of the country, but I established a rapport with the family which was to stand me in good stead for the rest of my time in Herefordshire.

The following week I had to be out of the house by 6.30 a.m. to muster with the rest of the workers at 7 a.m. The muster point was about one and a half miles away, and it meant walking through woodland in the half-light. Everything was quiet and peaceful.

The first thing the foreman did when we met was to look at my hands. He commented on the fact that I had not done manual work for a long time and suggested that I should urinate on them every day to harden the skin. I was learning the simple arts of survival.

I was the only Forestry Commission trainee, although a couple of months later I was told another trainee was joining the estate. I looked forward to his arrival as he was another ex-serviceman.

One Sunday a little sports car drew up outside the house and a chap in his mid-twenties got out. He was dressed in his demob suit, pork pie hat and lightweight brown shoes. He was an ex-RAF bomber pilot and even more unaware of the ways of the country than I had been. It appeared that he had no other working clothes or boots so I suggested that he needed to kit himself out.

The following morning we got him up at 6 a.m. with a struggle. It was pouring with rain. Bob found him an old hessian sack to keep off the worst of the wet. By the time we reached the muster point he was soaked to the skin. The foreman took one look at him and suggested that he should go back home and change into more suitable clothing. He disappeared at great speed. When I got home that evening I asked

Mrs Jones what had happened. She told me that he had packed his belongings and departed for London. We never saw him again. I had a certain sympathy for him, but I must say that the Forestry Commission did not brief their trainees adequately when they recruited them.

I stayed on the estate until November. The work was very varied. Thinning new plantations, cutting out and removing old standing timber, sawing up pit props, fencing, planting, cleaning. The work was hard, but very rewarding. We used traditional tools, axes, cross cut saws and bill hooks. The power saw had not been seen in Herefordshire at that time.

I became very fit and found that I could match the locals on output. Initially they were very offhand, but gradually I became accepted and was even invited down to the local pub for a drink. Honour indeed, but partly due, I'm sure, to Bob putting in a good word.

Sometime in early summer I was notified by Bangor University that I would not be able to take up my place. It had been decided, because of the large number of applicants, to increase the educational requirements from matriculation to Inter Bsc. Also I was one of the youngest ex-servicemen (20) and there were many older people who were married. My world fell apart. In vain did I point out to the University that I had already completed the first year of a two-year Inter BSc course before joining up.

I immediately applied to go to the Forestry Commission Training School in the Forest of Dean. I sat the entrance exam at Bristol in August. I was called back for interview and told that I had passed but was the youngest applicant and unmarried. Priority was being given to older and married men. How long before they would allocate me a place? Possibly two to three years – I felt I had travelled this road before.

Everyone at Byford was very sympathetic. Lots of beer was consumed to commiserate my bad luck. I really felt that

I was amongst friends. But what to do? I decided to stay on for the time being. However, fate has a way of taking a hand, and a few weeks later I received a telegram from Jack Reid. It said that there was a vacancy for a meteorologist on an expedition going to Antarctica. If I was interested, contact him immediately.

Surprisingly, it was Bob and his wife who really made up my mind. They pointed out that if I stayed on at Byford I would have to wait years to get to the school. I would become increasingly frustrated. Why not go off for a couple of years? I could always reapply to the Forestry Commission when I came back. It sounded good advice.

A couple of weeks later I said goodbye to all my friends and departed for London.

Years later, in 1992, my daughter Karen was on UK leave from QANTAS. She, my wife Joan and I decided to spend a few days exploring the Wye Valley. A few miles out of Hereford on the road to Hay-on-Wye I realized that we were near the estate. We needed to stop to find overnight accommodation so I went to the estate gatehouse and spoke with the occupiers. Amazingly, although he had not worked on the estate in my time, the man was a local and knew the Joneses and their family. Mrs Jones was still alive, in her eighties, and lived in a nursing home a few miles down the road.

We found the accommodation nearby. The following morning we drove to the nursing home and I asked if I could see Mrs Jones. A nurse took me up to her room, opened the door and said, "There is a visitor to see you Mrs Jones." She looked up from her book and said, "Hello, David. How are you?" She had no prior notice of my visit. I was amazed. I sat down with her and as we chatted the forty-five years since our last meeting simply rolled away. It was a heart-warming experience.

9

South to Antarctica: 1947

On the early morning of 18 December 1947, twenty-seven strangers started gathering at Tilbury aboard the newly commissioned *John Biscoe* expedition ship of the Falkland Islands Dependencies Survey. We were welcomed aboard by our leader, Dr Vivian Fuchs, who most of us had never met. The sight that greeted us was one of absolute chaos. Boxes, crates, drums and equipment of all shapes and sizes were scattered haphazardly across the quayside and the decks of the vessel. There did not appear to be a stevedore in sight. It was obvious we would be loading everything ourselves.

Our first priority was to find somewhere to bed down. There were two main areas, the first, amidships, accommodated eighteen, the second, aft over the propeller shaft, accommodated seven. This area could only be accessed through an after deck hatch down through a stowage space. Gradually we were organised into gangs by the ship's officers and started a somewhat half-hearted effort to sort out the confusion. Early evening we had a meal aboard and then repaired to a local pub and spent a couple of hours getting to know each other.

The following morning we had an early breakfast and set to with a will. Everyone, including "Doc" Fuchs, worked like Trojans. Eventually some order started to appear. We tried to identify and segregate stores for the individual bases. These were only identified by an alphabetical code so we had no idea where it was all going. By mid afternoon we felt we were beginning to win when a newsreel cameraman from Gaumont British News arrived to film us departing. Great panic ensued, we were not anticipating to sail until next day. So everyone had to hastily change back into decent clothes and line up whilst a film crew "panned" the ship to give the appearance of it moving. We had to shout and wave goodbye to a non-existent crowd of well-wishers. We thought it hilarious and it gave a lot of amusement to the various spectators hanging around the docks.

Unknown to us, the Captain could not get Board of Trade clearance to sail because he was undermanned. To overcome this he hastily recruited several odd characters from the local pubs and signed on all the expedition members as 'supernumeraries'. He got his Board of Trade certificate!

We continued to load and stow ship until late that night, had a few hours sleep and then started early next morning. By ten a.m. we were able to slip cables and steam away from our berth, this time with a genuine crowd of well-wishers waving to us. We had to substantially reduce the amount of deck cargo because we were deemed to be top heavy. This was no mean feat because the main problem was three massive crates, which contained our aeroplane and had to be positioned to allow free access to the bow area. It was surprising how many different points of view were vigorously expressed by a crowd of young men who represented all of the three services. However, the First Officer, who was a charming Irish peer called Lord H, used all his persuasive powers to get us to coordinate our ideas and efforts.

We began to take stock of our fellow travellers. I had been allocated a berth in the aft cabin. My companions were a mixed bag: Jack Reid, who had been in the Fleet Air Arm

The *John Biscoe* at Tilbury, 1947

with me in Hong Kong as a meteorologist (it was he who had told me about a vacancy with FIDS); "Jumbo" Nichol, ex-Royal Marine Commando who, by coincidence, had gone into Hong Kong the same time as Jack and I. We had never met. He had ended up as Provost Major in Kowloon with responsibility for "good order and discipline" amongst the dozens of brothels, bars, cafés and other dubious areas; "Junior" Scadding, an ex-Royal Navy meteorologist, considerably older than the rest of us; Derek Malin, an ex-RAF Pilot Officer meteorologist; Mike Green, a geologist, and finally "Dudley" Beves, ex-Foreign Office. He had talked his way into a free ride to the Antarctic by telling FIDS he was a correspondent with the *Times*. Having been accepted, he then went to the *Times* and said he was going south, could he be their correspondent (paid)? As he could talk the hind legs off a donkey, he got the job. We would get to know the others in due course.

The ship's official crew comprised First Officer, Second and Third Officers (both of whom had served on Atlantic convoys), and the Engineering Officer, a young Scotsman. He emerged from his hot, noisy and smelly engine room at odd intervals along the voyage to grab some fresh air and a cigarette. Other crew were the bosun, cook, four deckhands and several engine room 'monkeys'.

The ship itself was built in America as a boom defence vessel and passed over to the British as part of Lend-Lease. It's hull was timber pitch pine, 194 feet long, weighed 1,000 tons, and displaced 14 feet. Her twin diesel engines gave a maximum speed of 12 knots.

The mast was 70 feet with a crow's-nest which would be used for keeping ice watch when we got into southern waters. The luxuries provided aboard, which included iced-water drinking fountains (which never worked), a shower-room and large refrigerator, identified its American origins.

Unfortunately, in the rush to stow all the gear aboard, the ship's comprehensive toolkit for the engines was left behind at Tilbury. In consequence they had not got even a basic set of tools. This oversight was to cost us dearly later in the voyage.

By 22 December we had got everything stowed away as safely as possible and life started to settle down into a less frenetic routine. We were given lectures by either Robbie Slessor or Doc Fuchs on a number of subjects. Robbie, who was a naval doctor and a gynaecologist in civilian life, had been responsible for purchasing the first huskies in Labrador and Iceland in 1945 and served Stonington Island for the 1946 season. Some of the best dogs are bred illegally by crossing a husky bitch with a timber wolf. The female progenies are then used for breeding. They are a very tough breed, very good workers, if controlled, and tend to fight to the death amongst themselves. They are a pack animal having a King Dog who obtains and holds his position by fighting for it. The only way to break up a fight is to wade in and pull the dogs apart. They will not knowingly bite a human but in a free-for-all this can happen. The bitches are as bad as the dogs when it comes to fighting; they all like to sleep out in the snow, which insulates them, rather than under cover. As companions however they are unbeatable, they love human company. There were only two bases with dogs, Hope Bay and Stonington Island. The other bases were – in the main – used for weather observations and some fieldwork.

Doc Fuchs filled in the political scene for us. There had been a long-running dispute with, particularly, the Argentinians regarding the ownership of the British Antarctic sector. Britain had taken out Letters Patent in 1908 but the Argentinians had challenged this claiming that as the Falkland Islands and the British sector of Antarctica border Argentina they had right of possession. In addition, in the nineteenth century, the Falkland Islands were briefly held by them. They were, however, unwilling to take their case to the United Nations because they knew that legally Britain had a right to these areas. During the Second World War, both the Argentinians and Chileans had been active in Antarctic waters and currently had nine ships down there. Deception Island, on the northern tip of the Graham Land Peninsular, had been a pre-war Norwegian Whaling Station. It was abandoned at the outbreak of the war. Reports were received that the whaling station had been used by German ships during the war, so in 1943 a naval group called in there and destroyed anything of value.

In 1944 Operation Tabarin was mounted and fourteen personnel spent a season at two bases, Deception Island and Port Lockroy. The purpose was to show a British presence and to justify this by carrying out scientific research and operate a chain of meteorological reporting stations. Operation Tabarin was renamed the Falkland Islands Dependencies Survey as of 1946 and was now an ongoing presence.

The Argentinians currently had a couple of

meteorological stations in Antarctica and reports indicated that either they or the Chileans were proposing to establish more bases in the British sector. It was not clear how it was intended to deal with these but we were told in no uncertain terms that there was to be no fraternisation if we came across any strangers. We all thought it sounded a bit dramatic: after all World War III was hardly likely to be sparked off in the Antarctic!

Most people who had joined the expedition appeared to have been motivated by a sense of adventure and the desire to travel. Most had been in the services, had an active war and did not feel like settling down in the restrictive post-war conditions in Britain at that time. Everyone wanted to go to a sledging base but the only people who were guaranteed this were the surveyors, so there was a lot of talk amongst ourselves about who might end up where and with whom. Jumbo, Jack and I had teamed up so we hoped that at least two of us would end up together. As Jack and I were both meteorologists, there was no possibility of us extending our service together, which had commenced in 1945 in the Fleet Air Arm at Middle Wallop.

Christmas Day 1947 was celebrated in some style. The cook and duty mess assistant produced a wonderful traditional turkey meal with all the trimmings and a lot of liquor. We listened to the King's speech and wondered how we would celebrate our next Christmas on base. Most of us retired early that day.

Sunday, 28 December, the *J.B.* developed a major problem. We could only sail in circles. The control gear for steering kept on blowing fuses and the crew could not trace the fault. In addition there were no spare fuses aboard so the engineer had to improvise with bits of wire. It was obvious that we would have to go to a major port for attention as soon as possible. In consequence our original itinerary of calling at Recife in Brazil to refuel and water, and then on to Montevideo, would have to be amended. Instead we would detour to the port of St Vincent in the Cape Verde Islands to refuel and then straight down to Montevideo. I personally was very sorry about the change, as I had arranged to meet up with Phylis, an ex-Wren, who I knew in 1946 and now lived with her parents in Recife. This would now not be possible.

We arrived at the Port of St Vincent in the afternoon of New Year's Eve. The Cape Verde Islands are of volcanic origin with very little vegetation. The town had a backdrop of towering cliffs and ranges, the harbour entrance dominated by a sheer pinnacle of rock on which is positioned a lighthouse and radio station.

The crew of the *J.B.* and all FIDS were given leave to go ashore. We were warned that the town was an unhealthy place so to look out for muggers. Also we needed to arrange our own transport out and back. As there seemed to be no "bumboats" available, some of us cadged a lift with a coal barge. By the time we were deposited ashore, not at the main pier but at the Shell Oil Wharf in the native quarter of town, we were covered in coal dust. The crew of the barge started haggling over the cost of the trip and demanded an outrageous price. As we could see our drinking money disappearing rapidly we resisted. By this time a crowd of locals had gathered to watch the fun and things were getting uncomfortable. However, the five of us presented a united front and eventually the crew backed off and we escaped in one piece. We ran the gauntlet of falling into the pitch black, greasy water crossing a 200-yard narrow planking foot walk from the wharf to the main quay.

Once ashore we started walking in the general direction of the town followed by a crowd all asking for handouts. By good fortune, a local taxi came along so we flagged it down and all clambered in.

The local population were a mixture of Negro and

Portuguese but English was still the universal language (so we thought) so we managed to convey to the driver the fact that we wanted to find somewhere to get a meal and a drink. He assured us in some foreign language, and much nodding, that he knew just the place and off we went. He took us down a road that looked nothing like the city centre and stopped outside a large house. He went in and a few moments later beckoned us to follow. Inside we were met by a very large lady who spoke reasonable English and we asked for a drink and something to eat. The drinks arrived and tasted like firewater – it was cheap whisky. This was followed by a crowd of girls in various states of undress. It confirmed our initial suspicions that we had come to a brothel. We explained to madam that we were not interested in her girls and we wanted to leave. At that the door was barred by madam and the girls and they demanded to be paid. We refused and a pitched battle ensued. We made a concerted rush for the door and were not too fussy about manhandling them. Escaping into the street followed by a screaming crowd of women, we saw the same taxi parked at the kerbside obviously waiting for us. The driver had his feet up in the front having a doze. We gave him a rude awakening, piled into the car and, with a lot of urging from us, the driver got us away from the women, who were banging on the car shouting obscenities at us. So much for a quiet evening out!

We eventually caught up with most of the others in one of the bars in town and relaxed with whisky at thirty shillings (£1.50) a bottle, an outrageous price! It was obvious that it was also a brothel and soon a lot of girls appeared to help us drink. Eventually members of the party drifted away and left Jack, Jumbo and me in the bar quietly drinking our cares away. Apart from the moral issues involved, all three of us had by coincidence served in Hong Kong at the end of the war. We had seen the terrible effect of venereal disease on the careless or unwary.

Our pleasant evening was brought to an abrupt halt when a member of crew came in to tell us that we had to get back aboard as the ship had been refuelled and we were going to sail on the early morning tide. The problem was to find everyone. A number were obviously on the premises so we went upstairs to get them. We didn't expect what we found. In one large bedroom there were about ten of the boys in bed with their partners. One enterprising chap, Pat Toynbee, the pilot, had placed a mattress on the top of a large wardrobe and was settled down for the night. As one can imagine, none of them took kindly to our interference and Pat, for one, refused to move. Jumbo and I did no more than get hold of the wardrobe and tip it over. Pat and his girl landed across a couple of beds amid howls of grief and threats to perform unmentionable deeds to us when they got sorted out. Jumbo, Jack and I beat a hasty retreat and toured the town, which was not very large, tracking down the rest of the crowd. We came to another brothel and found the bosun downstairs, absolutely paralytic, drinking by himself, clutching a large piece of stone. I asked him what he was doing with it and he said he was taking it back for Doc Fuchs, who was a geologist. It looked more like a piece of road paving but I wasn't prepared to argue. Upstairs we found the rest of the ship's crew hard at it. They were very upset at being disturbed but so drunk that we were able to manhandle them off the premises. Jumbo was an ex-commando, a big strong lad, and Jack and I were quite nimble on our feet so that we were pretty safe. By some mischance, I carried the piece of stone back to the ship for the bosun.

When we finally came alongside the *J.B.* Robbie Slessor and Doc Fuchs were leaning over the rail telling us to be careful as there was fuel oil spillage on the deck. We all carefully, and, in most cases, with great effort, climbed up the ship's ladder and promptly slid over onto the filthy deck. Robbie and Doc thought it hilarious, so with my usual sense of humour I handed the piece of stone over to Doc. He asked me where I had got it so I told him "In a brothel," and staggered off to bed.

The following morning after breakfast, I was summoned to Doc's cabin. He demanded to know the full story, having already some inkling of what had happened in town the previous evening. I told him exactly but refused to identify the actual people we had caught in flagrante. What I did tell him was that the majority of the boys had been involved. He promptly put a P.A. out for everyone who had been ashore, crew and FIDS, to assemble on deck. When we were gathered, he read us the riot act. He had no intention of taking anyone south who had caught V.D. and he wanted everyone who had been with a woman to report to the doctor's for a medical examination. Everyone went away feeling sheepish about what they had done.

Unfortunately, that was not the end of the story. That evening I was called to Doc's cabin again and asked why I had not reported for a medical. I explained to him that I had not been with a woman, indeed, I was still a virgin. I had served in Hong Kong for a year and had seen just how low people could get. If I had wanted to have broken my duck I would not have chosen St Vincent. He then asked me why I had been in a brothel so I explained it all again. He was obviously unconvinced and ordered me to see the doctor. I refused on a point of principle, explaining that it was a matter of trust and he should be prepared to accept my word for it. I think it is fair to say that from then on I was not one of his favourites!

10

Arrival: 1948

On New Year's Day 1948 we continued our journey south to Montevideo. We had the usual "Crossing the Line" ceremony five days later. We were due to arrive at Montevideo in another ten days. The weather varied quite a bit but we got plenty of sunshine and painted the ship, making the *J.B.* very spick and span. The seas at times were quite rough and one day we were rolling 30° continuously which made life, in the galley particularly, most unpleasant. One thing we had plenty of was broken crockery.

On 12 January we got our postings. Jumbo and I were going to the Argentine Islands, together with Bill Thomas, wireless operator. This is a group of islands off the west coast of Graham Land which is about five miles distance. It was a four-man base first occupied by FIDS the year before. The islands had been the northern base of the British Graham Land Expedition in the 1930s.

The bright spot was that it was the dog-training base for the expedition. Jack was going to Admiralty Bay, a new base, with Eric Platt and Derek Farmer.

We reached the River Plate on 17 January and passed the masts and superstructure of the Graf Spee sticking out of the water. After docking we all went ashore to have a look around Montevideo. It looked like a North American city with skyscrapers and modern American cars on the streets.

Most of the city had been built in the last ten years. The shopping centres were incredible after London, full of clothing, watches and food.

Jumbo, Jack and I went to the English Club, a very colonial building full of expatriates who made us very welcome. They wanted to know about the expedition. We had been briefed by Doc Fuchs not to say too much because of the political situation so we gave them fairly non-specific information. We need not have bothered because the following day the newspapers were full of the expedition, its political motives, etc. Someone had obviously spilt the beans.

We found a restaurant which had been recommended to us by the 2nd Officer. It looked pretty dingy from the outside but the food was excellent. We had a pound steak, fried eggs and fried potatoes followed by fruit sundae and coffee. All for eight shillings! We thought it expensive but worth it. In the evening we returned to the English Club and found most of the others there. We had a very lively party and returned to the ship in the early hours.

The following day a party of us set out early for the beaches by bus and ended up at Currasco. The sandy beaches stretched for miles, the coastline covered with hotels. Tourism was the main industry. The morality squads were very active, strictly enforcing the "No changing on the beach except behind a screen" notices which plastered the area.

In the evening we visited the casino where we squandered some of our small capital. We walked through the city which was crowded with people dancing in the streets, watching open-air movies and eating in street cafés, and ended up at a nightclub. It was very dark and smoke filled with dim lighting and a floor show. As soon as our party sat down at a table, we were approached by girls who wanted to help us spend all our money. It was difficult to persuade them that we didn't want what they were offering. We noticed that Jack had disappeared but thought he had taken his girl off to dance. Suddenly there was a commotion behind some wall curtains and Jack appeared partly undressed, closely followed by two burly minders. He made a beeline for our table and pleaded with us for help. He had been lured into a room with promises of ecstasy and had promptly been "rolled" by the minders before he could even get into bed. They were demanding an astronomical sum from him and he couldn't pay. We all had a whip round but were just about cleared out. Things began to get nasty so we decided to retreat to the exit assisted by five or six minders in as good order as possible. They were kind enough to throw Jack's trousers out of the door as well. We had no money so had to walk all the way back to the docks. We got back on board the *J.B.* at about 4 a.m.

Not surprisingly next morning no one was interested to join me for a morning on the beach. It was our last day and we would be sailing in the evening. So I went off alone. I got on the beach and started to change behind an upturned boat. To my horror I was grabbed by a couple of morality squad heavies who escorted me off the beach into a police car and on to jail. Unfortunately no one at the station could speak English so I could not get them to understand that I needed to get back to the boat. Whilst they considered what to do with me I was thrown into a stinking cell to join a batch of drunks, perverts and thieves who had obviously been picked up during the night and were awaiting sentence. The women were kept in an adjacent cell and there was continuous fighting and screaming going on. I felt distinctly uncomfortable and a hardened criminal. The place stank.

By late afternoon, with no food or water provided and only a shared bucket in the corner to cater for bodily functions, I was beginning to get desperate. Fortunately when I did not return to the ship at lunchtime the British

Consul was alerted and he routinely checked with the police. I was released after a severe lecture by an English-speaking police officer who then kindly arranged to deliver me back to the *J.B.* by police car. Once again I was in trouble with Doc Fuchs for having delayed sailing by a couple of hours. Everyone else thought it a huge joke but insisted I had a shower and change of clothes before joining them.

Four days later we reached Port Stanley in a Force 8 gale and had some difficulty navigating the William Sound entrance to the harbour. To compound our problems we drew fourteen feet of water, which was too much to get alongside the jetty on an ebb tide. In consequence we ended up twelve feet from the jetty, stuck hard and fast. We had to rig a rickety plank bridge from the ship to get ashore. All this was watched by the Governor's wife who had come to welcome us in the absence of her husband who was south at the bases.

Our first impressions of Stanley were good. The town's population was about 900, half the total population on the Islands. The houses were built of granite or timber with corrugated roofs. They were all painted white, red or yellow and looked very much like a Scottish settlement in the Western Isles. There were no less than seventeen pubs or clubs, the Government House, a church, hospital and a small police station with no cell. Any lawbreakers, of whom there were few, were accommodated in a spare room of the police sergeant's house. The public hall doubled as a Magistrate's Court, when needed. The Falkland Island Company had a large general store and had the monopoly on everything imported and exported. I picked up a Parker 51 costing five pounds for Dorothy. Considering we only got paid seven pounds a week, it was a lot of money. I also found a very pretty dinner set made in England – export only – for Yvonne as a present. I cannot remember the price. We soon learned that this company was owned by absentee directors, mainly British, and this was the cause of considerable friction and irritation on the Islands.

A party of us, Dicky Laws, Derek Malin, Ken Pawson and myself, went off to climb Mt William, a 1400 foot peak about five miles out of Stanley. There was no transport so we hiked there and back. The climb itself was not too difficult but involved quite a bit of sheer rock scrambling with loose scree. It was grand fun and good exercise. The views from the top were magnificent. Returning home it started to pour and we arrived back at the *J.B.* soaked to the skin.

In the evening we attended a dance, which had been arranged for us. We had been warned that the local girls were desperate to get off the Islands and would do anything to get a husband. In consequence the event was a bit subdued but plenty of liquor was consumed. We also saw the police sergeant in action with some of the locals who got a bit out of control. He took off his jacket and escorted them outside where he systematically worked them over. He was an enormous man and weighed about sixteen stone. As there was no jail he sent them packing. We learned that there were only two problems on the Islands, drinking and sex. The first, too much, and the second, too little. Men far outnumbered women. The one punishment feared by everyone was to be "blacklisted" at the pubs. If anyone was caught providing drink to someone on the list they were fined heavily. From what we saw one had to be pretty far gone to go on the list in the first place.

HMS *Snipe* arrived back at Stanley with the Governor aboard on the second day. We spoke with the crew who told us that sea ice conditions were quite bad. They had damaged a bulkhead and sprung a leak trying to break out of Port Lockroy. They told us that the Argentinians had established two new bases at Admiralty Bay and Port Lockroy.

Later that day we had a briefing by the Governor. The political situation appeared to be degenerating into a farce with protest notes about illegal occupation flying about both ways. The Argentinian Navy was down in force and attempted to stop the *Snipe*, demanding to know what she was doing in Argentinian waters. The Navy gave a suitable reply! We were instructed to be very careful how we dealt with the 'enemy'. We finished off the day with a round of the pubs. We had a fantastic finale to our visit, everyone being very sociable. We even met up with some Norwegian whalers who introduced us to their national firewater, Ackravit. Three of these would guarantee oblivion. Somehow we all managed to get back to the *J.B.* in time to get underway early next morning. I discovered that I had brought a 'souvenir' back with me, someone's inscribed pewter drinking mug. Ah well! I would be making my humble apologies in the morning.

Overnight the gale blew up even stronger. Serious discussions took place between the Captain, Doc and the officers whether we should risk trying to get out of the harbour into open water. It was decided to go so we pulled out in the early afternoon and made the harbour bar safely. Once outside, one of the engines packed up due to contaminated fuel. There was nothing for it but to run for safety in Sparrow Cove. As we altered course we broached broadside to the waves which were horrendous. I was on duty doing bridge watch at the time and we watched the clinometers deflect to 48°. We could hear everything below crashing and banging. We thought the *J.B.* had had it. She hovered around for what seemed ages before slowly righting herself, shedding hundreds of gallons of water in the process. It proved one thing and that was the ship was a survivor.

We rode out the worst of the storm for about thirty-six hours and tried to sort out some of the chaos below decks.

A large generator had broken loose in the rear hold, slid across the deck and wedged itself against the door to our quarters. Luckily the wooden bulkhead held and a working party finally managed to shift it and lash it down again. Elsewhere in the ship everything was lashed down, tidied up or thrown overboard.

Together with *Snipe*, who had caught up with us, we headed for Deception Island. Forty-eight hours later we reached the Bellows, the entrance to the landlocked harbour. Deception is an extinct volcano comprising fused quartz and volcanic ash, very uninteresting. The remains of the Norwegian whaling station, partly destroyed in 1940 and finished off in 1943 by the Royal Navy, were still there; twisted metal and burnt timber, a sad sight. The outgoing wintering party were glad to be relieved. Jumbo and I met up with Frank Buse who was coming on to the Argentine Island for his second season.

The Argentine Base was situated further round the bay and an Argentinian Navy sloop had just landed stores to the personnel, who were all scientific. Apart from initial problems when they first arrived, everything was going smoothly between the two bases. Leave it to the boys on the ground, we thought, and not the politicians and everything goes well.

We stayed at Deception for three days off-loading stores. This was difficult because everything had to be rafted ashore and then manhandled up the beach. We were glad to get going again and headed for Signy Island in the South Orkneys. Full meteorological reporting was started and an ice watch from the crow's-nest was mounted. The first time I did ice watch I was on with Ted Gutteredge who 'froze' when he got to the underside of the platform. It was necessary to climb backwards and outwards to get onto the platform. It was not easy, especially when the ship was rolling. All I could do to help him was to get my head and shoulders in line with his legs and hold them tight. By

David at Deception Island

shouting encouragement to him I managed to get him over the problem.

We encountered our first large icebergs and the ship's speed was reduced to about 5–6 knots whilst a safe course was picked through them. I was on watch-keeping duties for several hours and got a wonderful view from the bridge.

Signy was reached late on the third day. The base was impressive, a gaily painted hut situated about 70 feet above sea level. The backdrop comprised towering peaks and snow-capped hills. What a contrast to Deception! The hut was absolutely spick and span and was a credit to the outgoing party who had been in the charge of Geoff Robin, an Australian. Dicky Laws, Derek Maim and Ralph Lenton were taking over for the next season. They would be able to do some climbing which made Derek very happy. For some reason we had the material aboard to build another base hut. It was decided that it was not necessary so we finished off-loading stores and left again for Admiralty Bay, where a new base was to be opened up. Two Falkland Islanders had been dropped off earlier by the *Snipe* and they were tenting

David

near to an Argentinian base which had been established.

We arrived at Admiralty Bay in driving rain and mist. It was not possible to get a view of King George I, which again is of volcanic origin. It took us three days to get the hut erected and shipshape. It was made by Boulton and Pauls, everything cut to size and numbered. Unfortunately quite a number of bits were missing so the spare hut from Signy had to be raided to replace them. Some of us took time out to have a look at the only salient feature on the island, a large glacier heavily crevassed. The Bay, in consequence, was continually choked even in summer by ice falls.

Saying goodbye to Eric Platt, Jack Reid and Dennis Farmer, who were staying, we pressed on to Stonington Island which was reported as ice locked. Fortunately, the Americans, who had just been into the base to break out Finn Ronne's ship, *Burton Island*, a sister to the *J.B.*, were prepared to wait for us and take us back into the base with their two icebreakers, the USS *Edisto* and USS *Port of Beaumont*. It was just as well they were there because we hit the pack ice a couple of days later. The captain decided to try and press on without the Americans but every time we tried to break a passage with engines running flat out we only succeeded in tearing off large chunks of the protective timber sheathing the bows. There was nothing for it but to wait for the Americans to catch up with us. We were stopped in Marguerite Bay and it was about another forty miles for the first ship to reach us. This was the *Edisto* which arrived in the early evening of 21 February and she steamed on ahead of us to rendezvous with the *Port of Beaumont* and *Burton Island*. We went alongside and tied up, the three ships side by side. Doc Fuchs went into a huddle with Ronne and Darlington, his No. 2 in charge and chief pilot. The rest of us wandered over the two American ships. We were impressed by the icebreakers, which carried helicopters, float planes and amphibious vehicles. The *Burton Island* carried two planes stowed on the aft deck. The ship itself had been ice locked all season and looked a shambles; gear was all over the place and it was in desperate need of a coat of paint. Rather like the *J.B.* when we left Tilbury only ten weeks previously.

The personnel of both ships were very friendly and treated us to things like ice cream and hamburgers ad nauseum. We learned that the *Beaumont* had cost £1 million to build and had five engine rooms. She worked on the principle of riding up onto the sea ice, the sheer weight of the vessel then breaking a passage. The sea ice into Stonington was about four feet thick so we would soon see her in action. The bows were sheathed with steel and knife-edged. There was no conventional keel and, in consequence, she rolled badly in heavy seas. All the normal creature comforts were provided: showers, cinema, ice-water fountains and excellent food. The crew did not seem to appreciate the wonderful scenery and wanted to get home as quickly as possible. They had been serving with Admiral

Byrd's Operation High Jump expedition. We were however very impressed with the photographic record of the expedition, most of it in colour. The expedition had been beset by problems due mainly to the bad weather conditions and they had lost a couple of aircraft. In consequence their time schedule had been reduced.

From the outgoing members of Finn Ronne's expedition, we learned of the bizarre situation that had developed at base. Ronne had decided to take his wife south with him and to appease the other personnel he agreed to let Harry Darlington's wife come as well. This set the scene for a most unhappy season, the presence of the two women causing a great deal of unrest, the women themselves not speaking to each other for the last six months on base.

The expedition's members were a very mixed bag and all seemed to want to tell us about the problems during the year. It had obviously been a very unhappy base, the bright spots being the field work which had been done in conjunction with the British team whom we still had to meet. The combined resources of the two bases and the sledging experience of the Brits had produced some very good results, including detail surveying of the east coast. The following day Doc and the Captain decided to try getting into Stonington unaided. There seemed to be a political reason for the Americans not taking us in but the rank and file were not privy to all the information. By midday, however, it was clear that we could go no further. Every time we tried to break a channel we lost more protective sheathing on our bows. We hoved to and waited for the *Port of Beaumont* to meet up with us again. As we were waiting, two sledges came out from the base, which was about three miles away. Ken Butler, the base leader, came aboard to confer with Doc Fuchs and the sledges returned to base with all the mail.

When the *Port of Beaumont* reached us she went on ahead

and took us in. In seven hours we offloaded tons of stores onto the sea ice to be sledged back to base. Before we left I managed to get ashore and have a quick look round the British and American bases. The British hut was very comfortable with a wonderful outlook over a frozen bay and glacier with a backdrop of towering snow-covered hills. The American base, on the other side of the hill, by comparison, was a shambles. The Americans had pulled out in a great hurry, left the base unsealed and treasure hunters from the American icebreakers had stripped the place.

We said goodbye to Doc Fuchs, Ken Blaiklock, Colin Brown, David Dalgleish, Robert Spivey and Pat Toynbee. We took aboard the outgoing personnel. They included Ken Butler, Doc Butson, Reg Freeman, Doug Mason, Ken McLeod, Bill Thomson, John Tonkin and Kevin Walton; also Frank Elliott, Mac Choyce and John Francis, all of whom had been in the Hope Bay sledging party. We headed north for the Argentine Islands. From them we learned more about their activities during the season. They all appeared to be well-rounded, mature characters with an easy camaraderie, somewhat different from some of the people we had taken off other bases.

From them we heard of the four major sledging trips that had been carried out that season, some of them in conjunction with Finn Ronne's expedition personnel, and also details of the survey of the eastern side of the Graham Land Peninsular by the Hope Bay team, who covered 550 miles and were in the field for seventy-one days with no support before reaching Stonington Island. We also heard more about the problems between the British and American bases and the internal factions that split the Americans.

It appeared that when Ronne returned to Stonington Island in 1946, having vacated the base in 1940, he was upset to find a British base there and his base hut vandalised. He would not accept Ken Butler's explanation that there had been visits to the base by both Chileans and Argentinians during the war years and they had caused the damage. Ronne insisted that, because of this, there was to be no fraternisation with the British. The British, on their part, were appalled at the presence of two women on base and predicted dire consequences.

The Americans were a very mixed crowd, some of whom were unsuited to the Antarctic. Those who had actually operated in the field with the British later in the season had proved themselves well. The no-fraternization ban gradually broke down as small groups of Americans crept away from their own base and visited their opposite numbers. They were amazed at the comfortable conditions and tidiness of the British base by comparison to the austere, windowless, unkempt building they lived in.

In time it was obvious this state of affairs could not go on and eventually Ken Butler and Finn Ronne agreed to carry out joint field operations together. The Americans had three aircraft but few dogs. The British had one aircraft and lots of sledging experience with several very good dog teams. They also had superior field equipment – tents, sledges and rations. From then on there was full cooperation between both expeditions.

These wonderful experiences could never be matched on a small base and those of us getting off at the Argentine Islands could only secretly admire and envy the luck of the men who served out their time on a sledging base. Jumbo and I both resolved that, if possible, we would do a second year at either Hope Bay or Stonington Island. On the 25 February 1948 we formally took over from "Dicky" Bird, Gordon Stock and two Falkland Islanders, Reeve and Watson. Our season had begun.

11

One Small Base: 1948

Our four-man base was one of several established during the period 1946–47 around the coastline of the Graham Land Peninsula, later to be renamed the Antarctic Peninsula. However, it was different to the other small bases, because we shared it with a group of huskies.

In 1948 Base F Argentine Islands had been established a year. It was a group of small islands five miles off the west coast of Graham Land. "Jumbo" Nichol, Base Leader; Bill Thomas, Radio Operator; Frank Buse, General Duties; and me, Meteorologist, took over the base in February 1948 from Dicky Bird and three companions. Historically, the Argentine Islands were the site of the northern base of the British Graham Land Expedition during 1934–37. No trace of the expedition hut remained in 1947 when a landing party came ashore to set up a new base. It was subsequently established that a tidal wave had destroyed it in April 1946. Our nearest neighbours were at Post Lockroy 40 miles to the north and Stonington Island 200 miles to the south.

We inherited a motley collection of adult dogs and half-grown youngsters. Three of the bitches were pregnant and were due to whelp shortly. Dicky Bird, the outgoing Base Leader and Meteorologist, gave us a quick run down on the dogs and their names, too many to remember but fortunately a register had been maintained. He also briefed

Frank's house

me on the meteorological equipment. The handover, of necessity, had to be brief as there was a great deal of work to complete before the *John Biscoe* sailed. Dicky was moving on to Hope Bay for his second season.

Our instructions from Doc Fuchs for the coming season were to continue the breeding and training programme commenced the previous year and stockpile as many seal carcasses as possible. The best of the trained dogs would be passed, together with spare seal carcasses, to the two sledging bases at Hope Bay and Stonington Island in 1949.

We knew from information given to us on the journey down from England by Robbie Slessor that the original twenty-five huskies were purchased in Labrador for Operation Tabarin 1944. A second batch of twenty-two was picked up in Labrador by Robbie in 1945. As he was a gynaecologist in civilian life he was amply qualified for the job. He had served at Base E Stonington Island during the season 1946–47.

Robbie had also told us about the pack hierarchal structure with a King Dog who established his position by combat and had good order and discipline maintained by his henchmen. However, as the lieutenants were ambitious to take the lead role, the King Dog's position was never totally secure. If he became old or ill, he would be displaced. Although Robbie told us that the dogs ate meat, seal or penguin, we never asked and he forgot to tell us how much they ate. This point was to become a key element in our lives during the next year.

Our practical initiation to base life started very quickly. As soon as the *John Biscoe* was hull down on the horizon on 26 February 1948, we were preoccupied with moving a mass of stores off the beach where everything had been dumped the day before. Because of the way the ship had been loaded at Tilbury Docks, not everything for the base was immediately accessible. Fuel, most of our food supplies, replacements for the radio equipment, and field equipment such as sleeping bags, were left on board to be offloaded on the ship's next visit. Most of the adult dogs were chained up to "dead men", pieces of wood which were frozen into the snow. These were either bitches on heat or members of the 'awkward squad' who were known troublemakers. As the area around base had been ice free, the rest of the dogs had been allowed to roam free during the day. Suddenly an almighty fight broke out on the dog lines behind the base hut. Rushing to the scene we were confronted by ten to fifteen dogs engaged in pitched battle and apparently enjoying every minute of it. We knew from Robbie's advice that the only way to break up a major fight was to wade in and pull them apart. This we did, confident in the knowledge that huskies would never knowingly bite a human (this according to Robbie). What we did not appreciate at that stage is that in the heat of battle it is sometimes impossible for a dog to distinguish between animal and man. When the battle subsided we discovered that the cause of the fight was one of the bitches in season who sat there laughing her head off. A couple of potential suitors had clashed and all the other dogs and bitches running free had joined in just for fun.

We held a post-mortem on the fight that evening. We felt that the dogs were aware of a change of personnel on base and were just testing the water with the new team. We also decided that the dogs could only run free when they could be supervised. We also noted that, however young, every dog seemed to want to become involved. There was obviously another side to these friendly, lovable animals.

Our next urgent priority was to sort out the feeding arrangements for the dogs. Huskies, like humans, want to be fed at regular intervals. If they are not, they become bad tempered! We had been told by Dicky that the dogs needed about 4 lbs of seal meat every second day. From the racket they were kicking up it was obvious they were hungry despite the fact that Dicky had told us they had been fed the day before. There were a couple of seal carcasses near the hut, covered over with a tarpaulin to protect them from the dogs. We knew that one full-grown carcass would last about three days, and that there was a stockpile of about twenty-five to thirty seals on Three Little Pigs, buried in deep snow to preserve them. There was open water to these islands so we would need to get the boat out and explore. Jumbo and I dismembered a seal under Frank's tuition. His uncle was a butcher in Port Stanley and he knew about these things. We had taken the precaution to chain up all the dogs before we did this, otherwise they would have made the job impossible. Once fed, the dog lines went quiet. Even the youngsters settled down for a while.

The following day, much to our delight, we discovered that Bessy had whelped in one of the empty crates. She produced six pups, two of them dead. She caught us by surprise, as she was not due to whelp for another week. This was her first litter and she did not appear to be producing any milk and the poor little creatures were desperate to feed. We decided to make up a solution of condensed milk and feed them by giving them our little fingers to suck. We piled straw into the crate, kept feeding them regularly and hoped nature would take its course.

Bill, in the meantime, was getting acquainted with his radio equipment. Whilst he was making his first transmission the generator packed up. This sadly was to be the overriding problem during the whole of our season. He had been warned by the outgoing radioman, Gordon Stock, that the equipment was unreliable but spares had been ordered which we knew were on the *John Biscoe*, so we were not too worried.

Two days later we fed the last of the seal meat to the dogs so Jumbo and I took off round the shoreline of the island by boat and sighted two Weddell seals lying out on an ice pan, a small flat floating piece of sea ice. Jumbo, who was an excellent shot, got off a couple of rounds killing one outright and mortally wounding the other one. The problem of retrieval proved more difficult than we had imagined. Rowing alongside the ice, I jumped out of the boat; the ice tipped and the seals started sliding into the water. By good fortune, I managed to get a grappling hook into one whilst Jumbo got a rope attached to them. Feeling very pleased with our catch, we towed them back to base where we were greeted by all the loose dogs who were wildly excited at the prospect of fresh meat. The dogs got their meat and that evening Frank, who was cook, rustled up a first-class meal of fried liver. It tasted a bit fishy and was very strong but we all enjoyed it.

The next day Jumbo and I made our first attempt to try some of the dogs in harness. We understood from Dicky that most of the adults were sledge trained so we anticipated that it would be pretty straightforward. How wrong we were! We decided to run a team of five. We thought that Duke, as King Dog and an experienced sledge, would be a good leader and selected the others more or less at random.

As soon as we appeared with harness, the dogs started to leap up and down shouting their heads off. Trying to get the harness on one dog required the efforts of both of us. As we finished each dog we clipped it to the sledge main trace. As soon as the second one was in position they started fighting. We broke the fight up and went back for the third dog, and fighting broke out again. It took us about half an hour to get them all in position and ready to go.

We gave Duke the command to go, "Wheet". He just sat there looking totally uninterested. Either he had forgotten the words of command or perhaps he knew we were both "rookies" and was testing us. Finally, by me dragging him forward and Jumbo driving the sledge and yelling "Wheet", we managed to get them all moving. The backdrop at the base was a hill with a fairly gentle gradient to the top, which was about 100 feet above sea level. The team took this quite well, all pulling together, but as soon as they got to the top they took off at the gallop. The far side of the hill ended with an ice cliff and they all headed for this, totally ignoring Jumbo's anguished cries of "Stop", together with a lot of unprintable comments. I was left a long way behind and could only watch in dawning horror at the thought of the whole lot disappearing over the edge of the cliff. The brake wouldn't hold them but at the last moment Jumbo managed to turn the sledge over. The handlebars dug into the snow and the headlong dash was halted. The sledge was badly damaged; a runner and the handlebars broken. Three of the dogs had slipped their harness and headed straight back to base. Jumbo and I got the sledge back eventually to find the three dogs sitting there laughing/smirking at us. We decided to run a smaller team next time and to learn something about repairing sledges.

Although we had only been on base a short while, it was obvious that the dogs would be a major priority in our lives.

Bonding was already developing. Frank and I had taken on responsibility for trying to rear the new pups of Bessy and Bunty. Neither bitch appeared to be producing enough milk so we continued our efforts to wean them on condensed milk. Initially the mothers did not like us handling the pups but gradually we were accepted, probably because they realised we were trying to help them. Sadly it soon became clear that not all of the pups would survive. Some of Bunty's were having trouble with their back legs, which appeared to be some form of paralysis. Jumbo consulted David Dalgleish who was doctor at Stonington Island. He suggested that if there was no improvement in a few days they should be put down. Frank, particularly, was upset as he was looking after these pups. When the time came he gently took them away from their mother, who did not seem to be too upset. I think animals are aware of illness and tend to reject the weak.

Shortly after this a third bitch, Monkey, produced five puppies, all of them healthy. She had made her bed in the store hut and, despite efforts to move her nearer the main hut, was determined to have them where *she* wanted. She

Curious puppies

148

was a very good mother, had plenty of milk and did not want her pups handled.

Dog training and sealing progressed in earnest through April and May when the ice between the islands was sufficiently thick to take sledges. Jumbo and Frank in particular spent a lot of time with the dogs and were beginning to get quite proficient at handling them. The early problems of harnessing up and uncontrolled sledging began to recede. We were restricted to sledging around the immediate islands because a lot of wide tracts of open water kept appearing out to sea and in the channel between us and the mainland. There were obviously strong currents preventing the sea ice freezing over completely.

Each of us had a favourite dog. Mine was a young bitch, a very sweet-natured lady named Polly. She had no real vice and kept apart from the other bitches, avoiding confrontation where possible. However, if she was forced to stand her ground she could give a good account of herself. She later became an excellent lead dog when sledging, being highly intelligent and able to "read" the surface well. She needed very little control by the driver, being able to find a good route through pressure ridges and rotten ice. As she was small for a husky, she found it very difficult to break a trail through deep snow and we would use a bigger dog on these occasions. Because she was so well behaved she spent minimal time on the dog lines and often used to sleep under the sledges, which were stacked by the side of the base hut. She would often accompany me on my meteorology rounds which involved checking the site instruments and ice conditions from the top of the hill several times a day. One of her favourite sunbathing spots during the good weather periods was against the sun recorder. In consequence on several occasions there were large gaps in the recorded hours of sunlight on days when there had not been a cloud in the sky. The explanation for these odd sun records caused a lot of amusement at the Port Stanley Meteorological Office when I turned in my weather reports at the end of the season.

I became very fond of her and later in the season was actively considering whether I could get her back to England when I returned home. Ironically she did come back in 1949, with a group of other dogs from our base, but died under tragic circumstances, of which more later.

By the beginning of April the sea ice was twelve to eighteen inches thick and seven-tenths covered. On 9 April, the SS *Fitzroy* was unable to get into the base because of thick sea ice. She got within four miles and could go no further. We believed she had offloaded our stores on the sea ice, anticipating that we would be able to sledge out and pick them up. Bill was unable to make contact with the ship so we did not learn what had happened until the following day, by which time the weather had deteriorated and large tracts of open water had developed. When we finally got out into the Penola Strait where the ship had been, there was no sign of the stores which, if they had been offloaded, had either drifted away or sunk.

Jumbo and I returned to base feeling pretty disconsolate and we all took an inventory of our stock. We had sufficient basic foodstuff left over from the previous year, albeit a somewhat peculiar selection which included tinned pigs' trotters (Who on earth had ordered them? we wondered), Libby's tinned mixed fruit, Australian tinned butter, corned beef, condensed milk and flour. There were only two 44-gallon drums of petrol to keep the generators for the radio equipment going and virtually no spares. This would probably mean that Bill would have to drastically reduce the number of daily transmissions and receptions. We were also without a serviceable rifle. We had a 12-bore shotgun with little ammunition and no sleeping bags, which would effectively restrict the amount of field work we could carry out. The one bright spot was that we had a small mountain of coke for our Aga cooker and heating stove. Things could have been a lot worse.

That evening we decided to "kill off" our small ration of alcohol, which comprised naval issue rum. The rest of our year's ration had been effectively removed by the stevedores at Tilbury who substituted bricks into the boxes. I think we even toasted them in our alcoholic euphoria.

The air temperatures were now falling rapidly and sea ice sledging conditions were quite good. Our sealing activities during this period were very successful and on one day alone at the end of April we bagged fourteen seals. We were working flat out to stockpile as many as possible before they withdrew further north to breed in warmer waters. Together with the stockpile which we had located on the Three Little Pigs, after a lot of searching, we were now assured of sufficient food for the dogs for the rest of the season.

There were now sufficient dogs sledge-trained to make three good teams. We found the easiest way to get the young dogs trained was to run them alongside their mothers in harness. With active encouragement from their parent, often a sharp nip, they soon learnt that it was easier to run than be dragged along by an enthusiastic team.

It was interesting to note that the huskies' approach to work can be rather like a human's; some would pull their hearts out, always giving their best effort. Others would do no more than absolutely necessary; they would keep their trace lines taut but did not put any real effort into pulling. And others would get bored and try and cause a distraction by jumping across the traces and getting everybody tangled up.

Jumbo and Frank spent more time than Bill and I did with the dogs as they were less restricted to base than the two of us who had to maintain regular radio and Met. schedules. However, because we were a small base we all had to take our turn as duty cook every fourth week. The other three would share the outside duties equally, which included feeding the dogs, sledge training and bringing in seals. Just to ensure that we were never idle the generating and wireless equipment was always giving trouble. Bill, Frank and I were continually taking turns to maintain the generator in order to stay "on air". Bill and Frank were good technicians and I learnt a lot about engines and radio. It was a question of making do with worn-out gear, trying to make up spare parts and maintaining schedules at a minimum level. We could not afford the fuel to use the lighting system in the hut so relied on Tilley lamps which were very efficient.

If we had previously held reservations about the ethics of Amundsen using dogs to get to the Pole, as opposed to man-hauling, we were now convinced he was right!

We had two energetic days actual climbing and managed to reach the summit of Mt Tuxen, but not without one or two anxious moments. On the fourth day we broke camp and started back. The conditions were no better and tracts of open water had started to appear. Our journey was lightened however by the appearance of about six dogs, including Polly, who had been released to greet us. They came streaming across the ice in fine form and escorted us back. Bill, who was cook that week, laid on a "welcome home" meal of substantial proportions.

The following day another series of depressions passed through and it blew hard for several days. When we managed to get out again to check, we found open water in the channel. We had been very fortunate to have had settled conditions for our trip and to return before the sea ice broke up. It did not re-form for several weeks and Frank and I would have been in some difficulty if we had been isolated on the mainland.

A final postscript was that I had taken a number of

photographs from the summit of Tuxen. The views had been breathtaking and the visibility was infinite. Sadly, when I developed the films there was not a single decent shot, due to over-exposure. This was a problem where there was a combination of sunlight and white reflecting surfaces. I was very much an amateur photographer with only a basic camera and a couple of light filters. An exposure meter would have been the answer.

12

Return to England: 1949-51

At Doc Fuchs' request, we reviewed our breeding programme to date. We had inherited three pregnant bitches, two of whom had produced dead or weak puppies. We had reared eleven but only three from Monkey were healthy. All the others were sickly, unable to suckle properly or suffering from what appeared to be malformation and paralysis of the hindquarters. Everything seemed to point to Igluk who had mated with both Bessy and Bunty. We had also lost several adolescents who were too young to be chained on the dog lines and were allowed to run free. Two just disappeared. We thought they had wandered out onto the sea ice, got marooned and probably drowned. Another was mauled by Hank, an adult dog, and subsequently died. The worst incident however involved Hilda, the first bitch to be mated since we took over the base. She could not pass the first pup and died in labour. This was a very sad incident and affected all of us badly. There was nothing that could be done for her and we felt totally useless.

Jumbo had several discussions by radio with Doc Fuchs and was finally instructed to close down the breeding programme. It would be taken on at Stonington Island. The advantage was obvious as there was a doctor on base who would be able to deal with the sort of medical problems we had encountered. The follow-on was that the base would probably be closed down at the end of the season and dogs and personnel moved to other bases. As the original reason for the opening of the base had been mainly political, with the removal of the dogs there seemed to be little point in maintaining it. This decision did not make any difference to us; we still had a lot of work to do for the rest of the season.

By early August the sea ice was again sufficiently thick for Jumbo to attempt his long-planned sledging trip. He and Frank had meticulously prepared all their gear. They were going to have to run a heavy load because we had no Pemmican sledging rations and they would have to carry seal meat instead for the dogs. This meant using a team of eight or nine dogs. They made up a new harness and had already made two very good sleeping bags using blankets and waterproof canvas. Frank and I had tested these out when we went to Tuxen and they had proved to be very warm.

The great day dawned for their start. The sledge was loaded, dogs harnessed, photos taken. They expected to be away for a minimum of three to four weeks, hoping to initially reach Cape Trois Perez about twenty miles to the south and then carry on as far as possible. Fuchs was looking at the possibility of a coastline survey south of the Biscoe Islands next season and Jumbo would recce the area. Later that day, Bill picked them up on their mobile 22 set. They were having to return because of open water which they could not bypass even by making a wide detour out to sea. They got back that evening frustrated but determined to have another go.

A couple of days later, after studying the sea ice conditions closely from the highest point on the islands, they decided to move off again. This time they were away three days but once more had to abort the trip because of open water and bad surface conditions. They had nearly lost all their gear when the sledge had broken through the ice. As it was, both of them were soaked trying to save it, but fortunately the air temperature was in the +20s so they made camp and managed to dry themselves out. I felt particularly sorry for Jumbo as he was very keen to achieve a really good sledging trip. The only good thing to come out of the exercise was that the dogs had performed very well. The hard work put into training them had paid off.

As thoughts of a long sledging trip receded we got a message from Doc Fuchs to say that Ken Pawson and two others were missing at Port Lockroy, a four-man base. We were to look at the possibility of getting a relief team up to George Barry, Base Leader and Radio Operator, who was alone and needed urgent assistance. The sea ice conditions to the north were very bad, the only possibility would be to work round the coastline in the hope of being able to cross the Gerlache Strait to Wiencke Island where the base was situated.

We realised that it would probably be a one-way journey as there would be little chance of our team getting back that season. It was decided to draw lots for the two to go. Just as we started our preparations Ken and his companions arrived back. They had been unable to get back earlier because of bad sea ice and weather conditions. They had been away four days. Everyone heaved a sigh of relief.

During September the weather was foul. Heavy snow and high winds obliterated everything and daily we had to dig our way out of the hut. A series of deep depressions passed through, temperatures plummeted and the sea ice in the channels was continuously on the move. Even in the worst weather conditions the dogs with their double insulated fur coats would snuggle down and sleep for hours at a time. They would be completely obliterated by snow and virtually hibernate. They would only come to life when we started preparing their food, all giving tongue together and making an unbelievable racket. They would also perform at night before settling down. The husky howl is a mournful sound and could go on for about half an hour. On a still night it was an eerie sound.

It was about six weeks before we could get the dogs out sledging. They were overjoyed to be out and working again and were very excitable. The situation was not helped by the appearance of groups of Adelie penguins on the sea ice which the dogs were desperate to reach. A number of different species of birds and penguins were sighted, a sure sign of returning spring. By October, however, the weather had deteriorated again, with heavy snow and low temperatures restricting outside activity.

By the middle of November, a lot of discussion took place across the bases regarding the next season. Jumbo was confirmed to open up a new sledging base on Alexander Island. I was going to Stonington Island which was remaining as a sledging base. We were both very pleased with the postings, but on the 26th of the month, news came through from Hope Bay that was to change all of these plans.

Whilst a sledging party was away a fire had completely destroyed the base hut. Dicky Bird and Mike Green had died but Bill Sladen, the doctor who was off base on a nearby penguin rookery, survived. In consequence the disposition of personnel had to be drastically revised. To add to the problems, heavy sea ice was reported from Stonington Island which was likely to prevent the setting up of Jumbo's new base. It might also put at risk the relief of the Stonington base itself.

The bad news from other bases continued to come in. Eric Plaff, Base Leader and Geologist at Admiralty Bay, was away from base with Jack Reid. He suffered what appeared to be a heart attack and died. Jack was unable, despite valiant attempts, to get him back by himself and had to return to find assistance. Eric was in his mid twenties and we could not believe he had gone.

Back at our base, December was a very active month. The return and nesting of shags on Galindey Island meant fresh eggs for us and we made several ski trips across the sound to collect as many as we could carry. Jumbo kept the dogs working hard, getting in as many seals as possible to stockpile.

Christmas was a great day. We all dressed up in our best "civvies", listened to the broadcast of the King's Speech and sat down to a first-class meal prepared by Bill assisted by myself. The menu read: Tomato and Oxtail Soup, Xmas Pudding and Tinned Fruit Salad, Xmas Cake and Mince Pies. It was brilliant and we finished off the last of our meagre stock of rum with coffee. Everything except the eggs, cake and mince pies came out of a tin. We gave the dogs extra rations as well: fresh penguin meat which they enjoyed enormously.*

It was nearly two months later that the *John Biscoe* relieved us. There had been various difficulties, including engine problems and heavy sea ice conditions to delay her. She was a wooden-hulled ship and was limited in her movements through sea ice. The first time she had tried to relieve Stonington Island in January 1948, she stripped most of the timber reinforcing off the bows in the heavy sea ice. She was only able to get in finally because of the presence of a US ice breaker in the area. Ken Butler, ex-Stonington Island 1946–7 who was FIDS liaison officer at Port Stanley, was aboard. From him we learnt our final movements.

---

* According to the British Antarctic Survey, small scale killing of wildlife for food, though not allowed today (2009), was acceptable at that date. "Seal steaks, liver, brains, heart, shags (e.g. Blue-eyed Shag – a kind of cormorant), paddies (Sheathbills) and penguins, including eggs," were all used to supplement their tinned and dried supplies. Could it be that the main course missing from the menu was something like omelettes?

Frank and I were going back on the ship to Port Stanley. Jumbo would probably continue for another year at the Argentine Islands if the new southern base could not be established. Bill would be going to Signy Island in the South Orkneys as radio operator; he was not very pleased with this posting. He would, however, be looking after some of the dogs from Hope Bay and our base until they were collected by a joint Anglo-Norwegian-Swedish expedition to Queen Maud Land. Frank and I made our farewells to the dogs and Jumbo and Bill saw us off early the following morning.

When we arrived back at Port Stanley I stayed with Frank's uncle, the butcher, for a couple of weeks awaiting passage back to England. I helped him make yards of lamb sausages; the residents of Port Stanley seemed very keen on them. I finally parted company from Frank and never saw him again. We corresponded a few times, the last after the Falklands conflict. Sadly he died in the mid eighties. It was the passing of a very good and likeable man who diplomatically kept the peace between the rest of us, at times no mean feat! We also had the advantage that, if we needed space and solitude, we could always take ourselves off to the dog lines. There we would get plenty of fuss and attention.

Fate, being unpredictable, decreed a change of plan for Bill. He arrived back in England in the summer of 1949 with the huskies, including my lovely Polly, which had been due to stay at Signy Island. What prompted the change of plan I cannot remember.

The dogs went to a kennels at Telscombe village near Brighton. Because none of the staff knew anything about the breed, Bill was asked to stay on to look after them. He contacted me at Herefordshire where I was working and told me he was back. I got down to Telscombe as soon as I could and had a happy reunion with Polly who was overjoyed to see me again. The conditions for the dogs were good and they looked very fit and well fed. Sadly, that all changed a few weeks later when an outbreak of Hardpad, a virulent strain of animal distemper, was diagnosed. As there was no known treatment at that time, despite the valiant efforts of the vet who ran the kennels, and Burroughs Wellcome who were called in, nine dogs died, including Polly. Because they had come from a totally sterile environment their immune systems could not handle the massive infection. To quote Bill Thomas who wrote at the time: "It's awful to see them fade away, the expression in their eyes is something that has to be seen."

It was a very sad time for everyone and seemed a terrible waste of such lovely animals. Their deaths however were not in vain. Burroughs Wellcome were able to develop a vaccine against Hardpad which was totally successful in preventing the disease. The survivors went South to Queen Maud Land and remained healthy.

Because Bill and I had unexpectedly come together again, we decided to go into partnership with the vet who owned Telscombe Kennels. We set up a new quarantine kennels at Haxted Mill, near Edenbridge, Kent. By March 1950 we were operational and were approached by ADS to accept a second batch of huskies coming out of Stonington Island for the forthcoming Festival of Britain in 1951. Stonington had finally been relieved, the first time for two seasons. The base was closed down and many of the dogs had to be destroyed because they could not be accommodated on the *John Biscoe*. This terrible task was performed by their own handlers with great humanity. Thirty-seven dogs were taken aboard the ship; of these a team of nine, led by Darkie, Fuchs' own lead dog, which had been inherited from Ted Bingham, were to come back to England. The rest were distributed amongst the other bases. This sad story is sensitively told in Sir Vivian Fuchs' book *Of Ice And Men*.

Bill and I built a special compound to provide quarantine

facilities, which had comfortable accommodation and a large exercise yard. We were assisted (when he was sober) by a "gentleman of the road" who arrived one day on his bicycle to which were attached all his worldly possessions. He claimed to be the son of a vicar and was obviously well educated. He stayed with us on and off for several months and lived in our straw shed. He had a primus stove and one saucepan which was used for both cooking and washing clothes. Even his socks were boiled! We attributed his survival to the quantity of liquor he consumed. When he did work, he worked very well. Then one day he took off and never returned. Bill and I often wondered what happened to him.

In July 1950 the dogs arrived at Southampton with Ray Adie, ex-Stonington base, in charge. He, like several others, had done three consecutive seasons in Antarctica. The ten dogs, including a couple of puppies Jane and Charlie, who had been born in transit, had a very pampered six months. They attracted an enormous amount of interest both locally and nationally. The press, sensing a good story, gave us plenty of coverage. The pups, especially, were very popular. Typically, they caused the most trouble, always into mischief and chewing up anything they could find. Leather collars were their main target and Charlie had to have an emergency operation to remove an internal blockage caused by a ball of chewed leather. The operation also revealed a couple of nails which had been swallowed at some point when I had been doing maintenance in the compound!

At the end of the quarantine period the dogs stayed on with us to be reintroduced to sledging. Jumbo, who by this time was also back in England, was recruited together with Ken Blaiklock, another ex-Stonington base member, to handle them at the Festival. Ken went on to serve again with Doc Fuchs on the Trans-Antarctic Expedition in the mid 1950s and did several other seasons down south as a surveyor.

Jumbo, Ken, Bill and I made up a couple of special sledges which could run on grass. Daily, the dogs would be trained in a large field at the rear of the kennels. This was also well covered by the media. In consequence, it attracted the unwelcome attention of several animal rights movements. Middle-aged ladies wearing tweeds and sensible shoes would appear with placards, protesting against the dogs being made to work. They would shout genteel abuse at us from the roadway alongside the field. In those days activists were well behaved and we used to regularly offer them tea which they always refused on a point of principle.

It was a very enjoyable period for everyone, including our kennel girls who adored the huskies, particularly the pups.

In due course the dogs were taken to London where Jumbo, Ken and a couple of others gave over 2,000 performances at the Festival. The public loved it and the dogs were very popular, in particular Darkie, who was a handsome black dog with white markings, weighing about 180 lbs. After the Festival Darkie went to Cambridge to live with Doc Fuchs. The others passed into history.

I am very glad to have had the opportunity and privilege to work with huskies in their natural environment. They are a magnificent and independent breed, full of character, energy and charm. Antarctica today is a poorer place without them.

Part Three:
Yvonne - Civvy Street

13

Back to Finchley: 1945-48

When I volunteered for the WAAF in 1942 I promised my father I would select shorthand typing as my trade. He was most anxious that I should not lose my speeds while I was away. However, I failed the trade test. The memory of my unfortunate experience with Japanese foreign policy at the Income Tax Collector's office was still relatively fresh and as soon as the dictation began my brain seized up. My pencil produced crazy pothooks. Given enough time I might have been able to make sense of some of them, but we were working against the clock. I had no chance. I tried to explain to the examining officer that I would be all right when I was in the job, it was just the test I couldn't do. He was not unsympathetic, but suggested I choose another trade. Which is how I came to spend four happy years in the WAAF as a photographer.

In 1944 I was posted to Whitehall, where, like Mollie, I found myself working in the warren of tunnels underground. My particular friend there was a girl called Pat. She was tall and slim, with red hair, hazel eyes flecked with green and an infectious laugh. Her ultimate ambition was to set up her own portrait studio, specialising in children and dogs. Her immediate intention was to apply for a grant when the war ended and go to college to learn commercial photography. I had no idea what I wanted to do when I was demobbed. I only knew what I didn't want to do – go back to live at home and work as a shorthand typist.

The European war ended in May 1945. There was dancing in the streets as the lights were switched on everywhere and blackout curtains consigned to the attic or the dustbin. Keeping in mind the fact that the Far East war still had to be won, people began to think of the future. Demobilisation had come one step nearer. Cautiously, Pat began to make plans. The first thing to do, when we were demobbed, was apply for a grant. I envied her certainty; I had no plan. Knowing this, Pat suggested that I too apply for a grant and if we were lucky we could go to college together. It seemed the perfect solution. Carried away with enthusiasm we talked of renting a little flat somewhere and being free and independent. Pat longed to break away from home as much as I did.

Father was deeply disappointed when I told him that after the war I wanted to stay in photography. He still had his heart set on my getting a nice safe office job and settling in for life. At first I thought he was going to insist on my returning to shorthand typing when the time came, but after a certain amount of argument and pleading on my part he agreed to let me have my way. In return I promised that if the course did not work out successfully I would return to what he still thought of as my real trade. I was so happy I would have promised him anything! I did not mention wanting to move into a flat. Time enough to cross that bridge if and when we came to it.

The end of the war in the Far East came so suddenly in the August that it took the nation by surprise. Pat and I applied for our grants and were successful. We were successful again when we were both informed that we had been allocated places at a photographic college in Bolt Court, just off Fleet Street. We thought our stars were riding high and were jubilant.

We came down to earth with a painful bump when we tried

to find a flat. In the drab post-war world flats were not only hard to come by, they were expensive. Too expensive for us, anyway. Our grants would not even stretch to a shared bed-sit. There was nothing for it but to go back home to live with our parents. It was a huge disappointment. However, determined not to be beaten, we promised ourselves that one day we would achieve our flat and – eventually – work together. It was something to aim at, to look forward to. We entered college more determined than ever to be successful.

At first everything was fresh and exciting, the work was interesting and I was happy. Then, as we settled down to a routine, two things began to worry me. One was money. The college fees were paid direct by the Air Ministry; apart from that I don't remember how the grant was made up. What I do recall was that after I had paid my contribution to the housekeeping and put aside my fares to and from home and college, I had very little money to live on. What was worse, I had no prospect of being much better off when the course was over. I would have to work as an assistant to an established photographer to begin with, a poorly paid job, so far as I could gather. In fact it would be years before I could think of leaving home – if that day ever dawned at all! Pat, of course, was in a similar situation.

The second worry had to do with the work itself. My practical work was good, but I was too slow. "You'll have to speed up if you want to do this professionally," one instructor told me. I tried, but the quality of my work deteriorated immediately. And I knew in my bones that I would not improve significantly with practice. After all, I had been developing and printing films for nearly four years. If I had not speeded up by now, I was never going to manage it.

Uncertain what to do, I told Pat of my dilemma. We were treating ourselves to soup and a roll in a small lunch bar near the college. As we perched on stools at one of the little round tables, I said, "I'm beginning to think I'm doing the wrong thing coming on this course."

Pat's eyebrows rose. "Why?"

"I don't think I'm going to get anywhere with it."

Again she asked, "Why?" and ate her soup while I explained. "What will you do if you pack it in here?" she enquired at the end.

"Go back to shorthand typing, I suppose. At least it pays quite well."

She glanced at her watch. "We're due back in just over ten minutes."

I gulped down my now lukewarm soup and scrambled up from the table.

The subject was not mentioned again until a couple of days later. Then Pat said over our lunchtime sandwiches, "Have you thought any more about leaving?"

"Yes," I said resignedly, "It'll have to be shorthand typing, I'm afraid. Sorry, Pat."

"Sorry?"

"We were going to work together one day," I reminded her.

Her smile was rueful. "Being realistic, do you honestly think we would ever have made it work?"

"No," I had to admit. "But it was a great idea."

"Yes. It could have been fun," she agreed. There was a pause while we mourned the death of our dream plan. Then Pat said briskly, "Well, if you're quite sure?"

"Quite sure." My tone matched hers.

"I was talking to my father about you last night – I hope you don't mind?"

I had taken a large bite of sandwich; with my mouth too full to answer, I shook my head. I liked her father. He was a scientist, working in the Department of Scientific Instrument Research, the DSIR. I had met him when I went to stay with Pat one weekend. A quiet, kindly man, he had been very sympathetic when I related the story of my disastrous test on Japanese foreign policy. I had hammed it up a bit and made him smile.

Pat went on, "He thinks that if you really don't feel happy with the course you'd be wise not to waste any more time on it."

I wondered what my own father would say when I told him that, after all my protestations, all the arguing and persuading him to let me have my own way over photography, I was going back to office work after all.

When I didn't make any comment, Pat said tentatively, "Actually, he says they're looking for a shorthand typist at the Department. If you're interested, he'd be glad to put in a word for you."

I was dumbfounded. The thought of going to work at the same place as her father and letting him down made me shiver. I said, "It's really good of him to offer, but I don't think I can go straight into a job without taking a refresher course of some sort first. I haven't touched a typewriter for four years."

"He knows that," said Pat. "He says they'd make allowances."

"And I'd be hopeless at the interview if they gave me a test."

"He knows that too. Don't you remember telling him you'd developed a nervous allergy to tests?"

I thought about it. Would I be able to cope with a job immediately? I had not forgotten my shorthand but my speed would be woeful. My typing would probably be even worse. I wondered if the DSIR realised just how many allowances it would have to make if it took me on. Still, Pat's father had thought me worth recommending and mine would be delighted. So why not go for an interview and see what happened? I said, "OK. I'll do my best."

"Good for you!" said Pat. "I'll tell him tonight."

I felt dazed. One minute I was merely thinking about packing in the course, the next I was being offered the chance of a job. I found it hard to concentrate during the afternoon. I was trying to think of the best way of breaking the news at home. I had never mentioned that I was in any difficulty at college; it was going to be a shock for them. I decided to dive in at the deep end, as it were, and tell both parents together.

I got home earlier than Father, so had to wait a while before saying anything. I then had to wait until Mother had served up the supper and Father had finished telling her about his day. I was still trying to think how best to broach the subject when Mother suddenly turned to me. "You're very quiet tonight, is everything all right?"

"I've been thinking about the college," I said. "It's not working out. I'm going to leave photography and go back to shorthand typing."

There was a flabbergasted silence. Mother looked exasperated. I could see her thinking, "Oh, no! What now?" But Father's eyes lit up and I knew he was pleased. He asked, "What made you change your mind?"

"The work. I'm OK as long as I can do it at my own pace, but I'm too slow to do it professionally."

"Who says so?" demanded Mother.

"The instructors."

Father was puzzled. "Nobody complained when you were in the WAAF, did they?"

"No, but that was different. The work there was only developing and printing and there's so much more to it at the college." (I did not add that even in the Air Force the ex-professionals had made rings round me when it came to speed. It had never entered my head that this would become so important.)

"So what are you going to do now?" asked Mother.

"I've been offered the chance of a job." I said, and told them about Pat's father and the DSIR.

Father asked, "Don't you think it would be better to take a refresher course before applying for a job like that?"

"Probably," I admitted, "but I didn't apply for it. It just happened."

"When?" asked Mother sharply. "You've never said anything to us."

"The job? At lunchtime. I never said anything about the course before because I hoped I'd be able to speed up. But I can't."

Mother was mollified, Father was pleased and I was relieved the ordeal of telling them was over. I had been pitchforked into keeping my promise to return to secretarial work if my dream plan with Pat failed. I had known I would feel miserable if it ever happened, but now it had I didn't feel as bad as I had thought I would.

Having admitted defeat the sensible thing to do was make the best of the opportunity that had so unexpectedly fallen into my lap. I took an illicit day off college to attend the interview. The DSIR had its headquarters in a tall, elegant old house in Russell Square; Pat, relaying the information from her father, said I would be seeing Mr Baron, the Head of the Department. I arrived early for my appointment but did not ring the bell immediately. I stood on the doorstep for several moments trying to control my nervous shakes. If anyone had come out of the house in a hurry we would have fallen over each other. Suddenly realising how silly I looked, I gritted my teeth and pressed the doorbell firmly.

The middle-aged lady who let me in was slim, with dark brown hair and eyes. Her features were sharp, but her manner was friendly. She introduced herself as Mrs Thomas, Mr Baron's secretary. "He's on the phone at the moment, but he won't be long. Please take a seat." A D-shaped table stood against one wall of the lofty hallway with a visitor's chair on either side of it. I sat to attention on the nearest one, trying to look cool and businesslike. Mrs

Thomas disappeared into the front room of the building and closed the door behind her. The house was very quiet. From a room at the back somewhere I could just hear the sound of a typewriter clacking away at top speed. My frail confidence sagged a little. It would be some considerable time before I could match that. I was glad when the door to the front room opened and Mrs Thomas invited me to come in.

I was facing a vast cluttered desk in a large room lined with bookshelves. Before I could take in any more, my attention became riveted on the handsome man behind the desk. Mrs Thomas introduced us and he stood up to greet me. Mr Baron was tall, with an almost palpable aura of authority; even without the introduction I would have known at once that he was The Boss. His voice was deep and attractive; his smile as he gestured towards a chair beside the desk was charm itself. I was completely bedazzled.

The interview was almost a pleasure. Mr Baron asked all the expected questions about my previous office experience, but made no reference to my time in the WAAF. The fact that I had been a photographer and had obviously wanted to continue with that type of work in Civvy Street was not mentioned. He finished the interview with, "There's no point in giving you a test at this stage. I suggest you come on a trial basis and we'll see how you get on." He named a starting salary that was a little higher than my grant, to be reviewed after a month if my work was satisfactory. I leapt at it, positively beaming with delight and relief. Another heart-throbbing smile was my reward. With magic timing his secretary returned. There was a short discussion concerning my starting date and she showed me out, also smiling.

Outside on the pavement I wanted to shout at the top of my voice, "I DID IT! I got the job!" That I was only on trial did not worry me. If I couldn't turn out a decent batch of letters by the end of a month, I ought to be ashamed of myself.

Instead of going straight home I went to the college. I felt an urgent need to tell Pat my news and thank her for setting the whole thing up for me. (I hope that in all my excitement I did not forget to send my grateful thanks to her father as well!) I was pretty sure that Mr Baron's failure to ask any awkward questions, or give me a practical test, was due to his influence behind the scenes. In addition I wanted to see the College Principal and start negotiating my release from the course as soon as possible.

It all took longer than I expected. I was late getting home. Father and Mother had almost finished supper when I walked in with a cheerful "Sorry I'm late." Mother was looking anxious, but her face cleared when she saw my beaming smile, "You got it!"

"Yes," I crowed, "I got it!" I was about to launch into a description of the interview when she stopped me. "Your supper's in the oven, keeping hot. Let me go and get it before you start." She swallowed the last mouthful of her meal and got up from the table. I aimed a kiss at her cheek as she passed me. Father was smiling broadly. "Well done!"

My elation soon evaporated. So did my self-confidence; my original doubts crowded back. Supposing I couldn't manage the job? Supposing I made a fool of myself and let Pat's father down? Supposing ... On the Underground travelling to work on my first morning I had to give myself a good talking to: 'Supposing you just stop supposing the worst and go and get on with it!' After all, the interview had turned out better than expected, hadn't it? The memory of Mr Baron's smile lifted my spirits and gave me something to look forward to. I arrived on the doorstep at the same time as a jaunty man with a key. He opened the door with a flourish and stood back smartly to let me enter first. I couldn't help grinning. Mrs Thomas appeared immediately from her office next to Mr Baron's. She said, "Good morning, I see you've already met," and introduced us to each other by name. His was Mr Harvey. "One of the men you will be working for," she added to me. One of the men? How many of them were there, for goodness' sake? My grin faded to a stiff smile as Mr Harvey said something polite and meaningless before heading for the stairs. Mrs Thomas led me towards the back of the house. The front door opened and closed behind us, light footsteps hurried to catch us up. I followed my leader into a room furnished for two secretaries: two desks, typewriters and tall metal filing cabinets. And the footsteps came too. Mrs Thomas turned and looked beyond me. "Good morning, Carol. This is our new secretary," and she gave her my name. "Will you look after her?"

Carol was young, probably straight out of secretarial college, with fair, flyaway hair, vivid blue eyes and a flawless pink and cream complexion. She reminded me of a china doll I had once cherished. However, I soon forgot my plaything; there was nothing doll-like about Carol apart from her looks. Hers was the fast typing I had heard as I sat waiting in the hall on the day of my interview. In fact all her movements were quick, and she was efficient with it. She was also unfailingly helpful, bless her.

It was a relief to find that I was working for only one man besides Mr Harvey. It had crossed my mind that the second man might be Pat's father. That would have been embarrassing. In fact I saw very little of him, unless we passed on the stairs or met in the hallway. My second man was a Mr Morrison. He was the old-fashioned gentlemanly type, though he looked too young for the part. His "Good morning" was always pleasant but impersonal. I found him rather daunting at first, but soon discovered him to be considerate and thoughtful for my welfare. Or perhaps it was the welfare of his letters? These contained long complicated formulas which he spelled out letter by letter and number by number, asking me to read them back immediately to make sure I had taken them down correctly. In my early days he also slowed his dictation down to a snail's pace for my benefit. I rarely had the slightest idea what he was writing about, but that did not matter. As long as I could decipher my shorthand (albeit with Carol's help) and type it back accurately, he did not question how long it took me.

Mr Harvey was, of course, totally different. He took a lively interest in my WAAF days and in his company I found myself lapsing into the slang of my service life. Some of it has since passed into everyday use, but it sounded very out of place at the DSIR at that time, and I was trying to forget it.

His speciality was glass eyes. There was a great demand for these by the end of the war. One day he took me down to the glassworks to see them being made. An intricate and fascinating business. Each one had to match the recipient's natural eye as closely as possible. I forget how they ensured the colour match, but I remember they took great trouble over it. Someone handed me a thin tube of glass about four feet long and suggested I try my hand at blowing a bubble. He held the far end of the tube in the furnace while exhorting me to blow into my end as hard as I could. I blew until I thought my lungs would collapse, but nothing happened. I hadn't enough puff to shift a feather, said the expert, laughing.

Mr Harvey also took me out for a lovely posh lunch that lasted far longer than the official time allowed for secretaries. During what was left of the afternoon Mrs Thomas, obviously disapproving, came in for a chat. She did not mention my overstretched lunch hour, she talked about Mr Harvey's wife. I knew I was being warned off and took it as a reprimand. I wondered how best to deal with the situation should it arise again, but it never did, although Mr Harvey remained as friendly as ever. I assumed that he too had been given a talking to by Mrs Thomas.

I rarely saw Mr Baron. When we did meet I was still treated to the same brilliant smile but it was vague, as if he couldn't quite remember who I was. Even when my month's trial period was up he was not the one who told me I had now been accepted as permanent. Nor did he tell me I was getting a pay rise. He left all that sort of thing to Mrs Thomas. Thinking about it afterwards, I speculated as to how it came about that he saw me himself when I came for my interview. I could only suppose he did it out of courtesy to Pat's father.

Although I quite enjoyed the job I hated the travelling to and from work. It involved a bus and Underground journey and took ages, especially in the evenings. When I came out of the Underground at Holloway Road station, there was always a fight for the bus, the losers having to wait for the next one, whenever that might be. The idea of queuing had never caught on at Holloway Road, where it was the custom to stick out your elbows and push. After a couple of years I was fed up with it. I wanted something nearer home.

I was beginning to think seriously of making a move when word went round the office that ground-shaking changes were in the offing. The DSIR was leaving Russell Square and going to Bromley in Kent, where it would be known as SIRA, the Scientific Instrument Research Association. Thus my mind was made up for me by the force of circumstance. I stayed until the office in Russell Square closed. Carol, if I remember rightly, went with them to their new premises. Pat's father was delighted with the move. As the family lived at Addiscombe it cut his travelling time in half.

I had been keeping an eye on the Situations Vacant columns in the local papers for some weeks without success. There was nothing much in my line at all. Certainly nothing that attracted me. I therefore crossed my fingers for luck and went into the secretarial agency nearest home. The manageress was pleasant and helpful, but had very little on her books at that moment. A lowly paid job as a pool typist in a building society was the best she could offer. "But call in again, something's bound to turn up soon."

"The trouble is," I confided, "I can't afford to wait."

The manageress had a suggestion to make. "Have you thought of doing temporary work for the time being?"

I hadn't, but I thought about it now.

Seeing my hesitation, she said, "If you don't mind what it is, I could fix you up tomorrow."

I had still been hoping for a job dealing with people. However, I had to face reality. I couldn't afford to be choosy. I thanked her and accepted.

'Temping' kept me in funds for months. The jobs varied from sitting at a desk at the back of a posh car showroom, trying to look busy with nothing to do, to working part-time for a lady solicitor who practised from home. I look back on this as my worst job ever.

The work was mostly conveyancing. Very boring! Added to which the files were always in a muddle. Being unfamiliar with the work, I wasted a lot of time trying to sort them out.

The solicitor had two small children who were not supposed to invade my "office" – normally the sitting room – but frequently did, pawing at the things on my desk with sticky fingers. If shooed out by their mother, they played noisy games in the hallway outside my door, bumping against it or rattling the handle every few minutes. From their point of view they were not invading my office, I was invading their playroom and they resented it. The younger one would sometimes bring in her potty and put it down beside me to perform on it. "Wee-wees" were distracting enough; "poos" were even worse.

The solicitor never apologised for her children or

reprimanded them. Neither did she like me protesting about their behaviour. In fact she complained one day at the small amount of work I had produced. I told her I would be leaving at the end of the week. She was quite put out!

14

Highgate: 1948 onwards

I called in to the agency to tell the manageress I was packing in the solicitor's job. She did not ask me why, or seem surprised. She said she had nothing else to offer me at the moment, but would get in touch when she had. I was a bit worried that I might have blotted my copybook. It was a relief when someone from the agency phoned one morning the following week to ask if I could go down to Highgate immediately. The job was an emergency, with another solicitor working solo, a Mr Bartholomew. He had been let down by his secretary and was desperate. I jumped at it, fingers crossed, hoping that he would be better organised professionally than the lady with the rowdy children. At least Mr Bartholomew had a proper office.

This turned out to be a small converted shop in a row of old-fashioned little shops near the Highgate Magistrates' Court. When I pushed open the door I expected a bell to clang above it. But behind the painted-out window, with the solicitor's name and profession scrolled across it in black and gold, I found a reception area-cum-secretaries' office. There was just enough space to accommodate two desks and a small switchboard. A short row of chairs stood against the side of a steep staircase leading to the upper floor.

The receptionist behind the switchboard, a girl of about my own age, with an unruly mop of auburn curls, beamed when I told her the agency had sent me. "Thank heavens! He's been doing his nut. I'll tell him the cavalry's arrived." She rang his extension and reported gaily, "Good news. The temp's arrived." Then turning back to me, "He says to go straight up. Come on! I'll show you." I dumped my coat on one of the chairs and followed her up the narrow stairs. On the landing she knocked on the nearest door. A commanding voice called, "Come!"

My guide threw open the door and announced, "This is—" before remembering that she had not asked my name. I supplied it for her and she grinned. Mr Bartholomew's professional smile changed to one of amusement. He stood up and leaned across his desk to shake my hand. He was a fairly tall, heavily built man with thinning dark hair, aged around fifty, at a guess. He asked, "Have you worked for a solicitor before?"

I was pleased to be able to assure him that I had and his relief was obvious. I was equally relieved that he didn't ask for details. Instead he glanced hastily at his watch and muttered, "I'm going to be late." The receptionist ushered me out.

Back downstairs, she chuckled, "I should have asked you your name before. Sorry about that. I'm Dorothy, by the way. Usually called Dotty." With her wild hair and seemingly haphazard approach to her job, I thought her nickname suited her perfectly.

After showing me where to hang my coat, Dotty got down to business. Two stacks of files leaned up against 'my' typewriter.

"I've sorted out the files for you," said Dotty. "The pile on the right is all bread-and-butter stuff. All they need is a holding letter. You know the sort of thing, 'Thank you for yours of whatever-it-is, which will be dealt with as soon as I can get round to it.' You'll find plenty of carbons on the files to work from. They need doing first. I'll go through the other lot with you when you get to them."

I was impressed. Dotty was more efficient than I would have given her credit for.

"There's one thing I ought to warn you about," she added, "Barty's got a thing about tidy files. He goes mad if the corners aren't exactly square, or documents aren't neatly folded."

"Goodness! What happens if you do something really serious?"

"Nothing!" said Dotty. "It's weird. He just says, 'Oh well, it's done now' and that's the end of it."

We heard Barty's door being flung open, he came pounding down the stairs and almost ran out of the door, letting it slam behind him. Dotty commented cheerfully, "He's cut it a bit fine this time. I hope he's not supposed to be on first."

We got down to work. At first I found it distracting when a client called in, or Dotty was on the phone, but I soon learned to tune out the interruptions. None of the files dealt with conveyancing. I queried this with Dotty.

"Barty only does court work," she explained. "He has a partner with his own offices. They do all the other stuff from there."

I thanked my lucky star that it was this partner I had been sent to and not the other one. I had previously decided that I didn't like conveyancing.

I had just reached the stage when I could have killed for a cup of coffee, when the door opened and a middle-aged lady with a pleasant face blew in on a gust of apologies. "I'm so sorry I'm late. You must be gasping. It's been one of those mornings. Everything's gone wrong."

Dotty said, "Good morning, Mrs Bartholomew. This is—" and this time she introduced me properly. My employer's wife smiled hello and asked, "How do you like your coffee? Or would you prefer tea?"

I settled for coffee and was offered a biscuit to go with

it. When Mrs B. had departed to her own room upstairs I asked Dotty what she did apart from making coffee.

"The accounts, banking, petty cash. Anything to do with the money side of things. She doles out our wages too," she informed me.

At lunchtime we both produced a packet of sandwiches and ate them at our desks. If anyone came in Dotty hid hers in her desk drawer, sat up straight and looked alert. There were also several telephone calls. "Have you ever worked a switchboard?" asked Dotty. I shook my head. "Well, now's your chance to learn. You can take the next call." I suppose I looked uneasy, for she added, "It's quite simple, I'll show you."

After lunch, an elderly lady, whose name I have forgotten, came in to do any copy-typing required. Statements for the Court and so on. Her room was upstairs, next to Barty's.

The only other member of staff was an articled clerk. "He's at the High Court today, attending Counsel. We don't see much of him, thank goodness. Cocky young so-and-so." I gathered from her tone that she didn't like him.

I ventured a question, expecting something vaguely scandalous in reply. "What happened to the regular secretary?"

"Mary? Her appendix blew up last night. Her mother rang to say she's in hospital."

I thought the agency's comment "he's been let down by his secretary" was a bit harsh under the circumstances.

Barty returned from the Magistrates' Court in the early afternoon and I was called up to his office to take dictation. He worked fast. I only just about kept up with him. However, he told me as we went along which files he wanted done that afternoon, so I knew he was not expecting me to do the lot before I went home. Which was just as well. I was secretly dismayed at the amount he gave me.

"Is it always like this?" I asked Dotty when I got back to my desk.

"We're always busy, but it's not usually quite such a scramble as this," she said. "But Mary wasn't feeling well yesterday and she left quite a lot of stuff undone. Some of it's had to be re-dictated. I wouldn't be surprised," she went on, "if she didn't come back. She had quite a long way to come and she was finding it a bit too much for her. She's been talking about looking for something nearer home for weeks."

I was dog-tired when I got home that night, but felt I had had a good day. I could settle quite happily into this job if Mary didn't come back. I would enjoy working for Mr Bartholomew. I liked his style. I knew where I was with him and felt I could cope.

Several weeks passed. The work was interesting; no two days were the same. The divorces varied enormously. Some were bitterly contested; some had obviously been sorted out behind the scenes beforehand by the contestants themselves. In these cases the solicitors had to be very careful not to become involved in collusion.

Dotty was right about Mary. She didn't come back. As I had hoped, I was offered the job permanently and accepted eagerly. It fulfilled my ambition to work with people. Or at least came as near to it as I was ever likely to get.

Not long afterwards our articled clerk didn't come in one morning and did not ring up to explain why. At coffee time Dotty mentioned this to Mrs B., who went all tight-lipped and said he would not be coming back. We never found out why Barty suddenly decided to get rid of him. While we were waiting for a new clerk to be appointed, we had no one to attend Counsel in the High Court; Barty had to go himself. The second time this happened he took me with him to show me the ropes. I went with a certain amount of trepidation, knowing that next time the occasion arose I would be sent on my own.

'Attending Counsel' sounded rather grander than it actually was. During the hearing the Solicitor's Clerk sat behind Counsel with all the documents prepared by the Solicitor – the Exhibits. Each Exhibit had been given a letter of the alphabet, starting, of course, with "A". When Counsel wished the Judge to see Exhibit "A" he did not turn round, he held out his hand in the general direction of the Clerk, who placed the document into it. And so on through the alphabet. All quite simple as long as the papers were in strict order. Counsel turned round quickly enough if he (or she) was handed the wrong Exhibit, and the look he gave the poor clerk was enough to make him shrivel in his shoes. I did not have to go up to the High Court very often, for which I was thankful. Although I never received "the look" from Counsel, I was always on edge in case I made a mistake. Which is probably why I can remember so little about the cases being heard. I was concentrating all my attention on Counsel and the Exhibits.

I settled in the job as happily as I thought I would and continued to live at home. Getting acclimatised to being the daughter of the house again had not come easy at first, but after an initial period of unrest I had settled down there too.

We did not see much of David, still at Haxted Mill. It was not until he bought a car some time later that he was able to get home easily. Our parents never acquired such a luxury and there was no question of our visiting him. In fact, thinking about it now, he and I saw very little of one another after I left home in our teenage years. However, in our different ways we could both look back nostalgically on a happy childhood in Finchley.

Lightning Source UK Ltd.
Milton Keynes UK
16 September 2009

143813UK00001B/7/P